Wolves
in Sheep's Clothing

Wolves
in Sheep's Clothing
A PONZI SCHEME VICTIM'S STORY

Pat Dougherty

PALMETTO
PUBLISHING
Charleston, SC
www.PalmettoPublishing.com

Hardcover ISBN: 9798822980310
Paperback ISBN: 9798822963870
eBook ISBN: 9798822980327

Foreword

This book is dedicated to those who have been affected by the lies and manipulations of Paul Croft and JD Frost. I hope that telling my story will expose these two for the con artists that they are while helping to make sure that they can never cheat anybody out of anything ever again!

Pat D

Introduction

In early spring of 2021, the Covid Pandemic was still a big part of everyday life and I, like most Americans, was working exclusively from home. I was 61 years old and had just passed the 28th anniversary with my company. Early in my career I had set a goal of 30 years and out which put my retirement date at June 1st 2023, but with the stresses of the pandemic and the situation with working from home wearing on me I reached out to HR and, when I discovered that the difference between retiring in December of 2022 vs June of 2023 was less than $40.00 per month, I decided to pull the trigger six months earlier than planned.

So, after 50 years of working, I put a big red X on December 1st 2022, and started preparing for the next chapter of my life! That's when I was approached with an investment opportunity and put in touch with Paul Croft and JD Frost!

Background

I grew up in a small farming community in Western Wisconsin, about an hour's drive from the Twin Cities Metro Area. I have three brothers, six sisters, and I'm number eight in the line of 10. When I was six years old my mother passed away due to complications from childbirth, and roughly a year later my father was diagnosed with cancer. He passed away 12 days before my 16th birthday in 1975.

My dad was a WW2 veteran who served as a supply specialist stationed in the Aleutian Islands and later spent almost 30 years working for the United States Postal Service. After he contracted cancer, myself and my younger siblings were raised on his social security and veterans benefits which provided the basics, but if we wanted anything extra, we had to work for them.

By the time I was seven or eight years old I was mowing lawns and shoveling snow, at 10 I had a paper route, I spent my teen years doing farm work while also bussing tables and washing dishes in local restaurants and diners, and even though I had the opportunity for a fully paid four years of college through my father's veteran's benefits, I went straight into the workforce after high school and did everything from light assembly, to meat processing, printing press operating, and ship building until I finally settled into a corporate customer service job where I would spend 30 years until retirement, during which time I went to night school to get my Bachelor's Degree in Managing Information Systems.

I got married at 30, had my daughter at 32 and my son at 34, got divorced at 42, and have been single ever since. I have two grandsons, three granddaughters, and both of my kids are doing well which makes me very happy!

My Friends

Some good friends of mine, a married couple that I had worked with for several years, had taken early retirements from the company to take management positions with another firm. They were both in the late 50s and were leaving six figure annual salaries, so their retirements caught me a bit off guard. But I soon found out that they were going to work for a clean energy start up called Rhino Onward International, otherwise referred to as ROI.

Not long after, they approached me with a ground floor opportunity to invest in a hydrogen plant that was going to be built in Arizona. Being a firm believer in renewable energy sources I knew that there was great potential for high yield returns in this growing industry, and the fact that my two friends, who I had known for years and trusted, had left good paying jobs to work for this company, I figured that this was something I needed to seriously look into, so I set out to do some research into the company and its principal investors.

Research

The first thing I looked at was the ROI Website: "Welcome to Rhino Onward International" the headline ribbon read, "We create the greenest and cleanest cradle-to-grave renewable energy by harvesting Solar Energy and Brackish (non-potable) water to generate electricity, green hydrogen, and clean water" and listed Paul Croft as the company's President and Jonathan (JD) Frost as the company's Vice President.

Who is Rhino Onward International?

ROI is a design-build developer as well as an integrator for our clients along with being a manufacturer of green energy solutions. Within our solar portfolio we manufacture CSP and PV, within our hydrogen portfolio/electrolysis we manufacture alkaline, PEM and SOEC (high temperature) along with water desalination.

ROI is a developer and owner/operator of its facilities or can be a turnkey green energy integrator for our clients for them to operate.

Regardless of which solution we choose, our main focus is helping our clients reach their decarbonization goals

Whether our designs use CSP or PV we harvest free solar energy which we use to produce clean electricity and water. We can then use that electricity to produce green hydrogen as either an energy product to use or as a dense form of energy storage.

My next task was to get more information on Paul Croft and JD Frost.

Paul Thomas Croft grew up in Two Harbors Minnesota and was 40 years old. After graduating high school in 1999, he studied accounting and business at the University of North Dakota, and after graduation he became a salesman with the Northwestern Mutual Insurance Company where his biography says he quickly became the 6th ranked rep out of approximately 1,500 financial professionals in the country.

Croft started his own accounting company, Croft Enterprises, in 2008, and a decade later Croft Enterprises would merge with JD Frost & Associates to become Croft & Frost. Croft was very active on several social media outlets and at one point claimed to be worth $700M.

40-year-old Jonathan David Frost, otherwise known as JD, was born into a very wealthy family who own and operate the global, multimillion dollar, Tuftco Corporation which claims to be the only company in the world that can supply a carpet mill with all the necessary machinery to take yarn from the tufting process all the way through to finished carpet. Their headquarters are in Chattanooga, TN, but according to their website they also have facilities located in the state of Georgia as well as OUS locations in Turkey, China, India, and England. A quick Google search shows Tuftco's annual revenue is $27.9M with the Frost family's net worth at roughly $50M.

The non-profit Frost Family Foundation of Signal Mountain, TN, shows assets of $9.9M as well.

From one of JD's many social media pages: JD Frost is the founder and CEO of Croft & Frost, a firm that transcends traditional accounting and wealth creation. With both a CPA and his MBA, JD advises businesses on more than just their financials: he utilizes four foundations of wealth creation to help his clients, partners, and employees build courage and create wealth. As an entrepreneur, he knows what it takes to start – and scale – a business, and has used his years of experience in accounting to build a solid foundation for each and every one of his clients and businesses.

I did multiple internet searches on both of these individuals, and their businesses, and found nothing to be alarmed about.

The Better Business Bureau gave Croft & Frost Accounting A+ ratings for both their Chicago and Minneapolis offices, they both had multiple motivational speaking videos online, JD had written a book about how to reach your financial goals, and they also both had online videos proclaiming their deep faith in God.

Weighing all of this and combining it with the assurances from my friends had me feeling pretty good about this opportunity, so I agreed to a conference call with JD Frost.

The Pitch

The call took place in June of 2021, and was attended by my-self, my two friends (who, again, were employed by Croft & Frost), and JD Frost. During the call, JD offered me a five-year investment deal that would pay me 100% interest for year one, basically doubling my investment of $250,000 to $500,000, and 12% annually for the next four years with a balloon payment of $740,000 in 2026. I expressed to JD that the only investment I could make had to have a monthly payout component in order for it to work because I needed that to supplement my pension and social security. He then offered me the following investment structure.

$250,000 investment – 100% interest year one, doubling to $500,000. Then 12% interest years 2-5, with 8% being paid in 48 monthly installments of $3400 with the remaining 4% accruing on the principal balance.

$250,000 - $500,000
48 payments of $3400 = $162,200
Balloon payment of $580K to be paid in 2026
Total payout on investment = $743,200

Even though these numbers sounded too good to be true, I had been a proponent of renewable energy sources for some time and knew that the industry was growing by leaps and bounds! I also knew that there was great potential for high yield returns in this growing industry and the fact that my two friends, who I had known for years and trusted, had left good paying jobs to work for this company, I figured that this investment was something I needed to seriously think about, so I told JD that I would get back to him and after a couple weeks of contemplation I made the decision to invest in Rhino Onward International.

The Buy In/Investment (IRA Club)

A promissory note was drawn up stating the Terms of the Agreement and sent to me via DocuSign. As you can see by the screenshot provided it was signed by Paul Thomas Croft.

I was put in contact with a man named Carlos at the IRA Club in Chicago, IL. They would be the holders of the promissory note and it would be their responsibility to process the monthly payments of $3400 from Taurus LLC, take out federal taxes (20% at my direction), and directly deposit $2710 into my bank account every month. I paid $5.00 to set up an IRA Club account and once everything was signed and sent, I directed my investment group to send me a cashier's check for $250,000 which I gave to my friends who, in turn, sent it to Paul Croft and JD Frost. So, the investment was made and we were set to go.

Below is a copy of the promissory note.

PROMISSORY NOTE

St. Paul, Minnesota
August 12, 2021

$250,000.00

FOR VALUE RECEIVED, the undersigned, **TAURUS V, LLC**, a Nevada limited liability company ("Borrower"), hereby promises to pay to the order of **IRA Club FBO Pat Dougherty IRA 1002798**, 614 Spruce Dr. Hudson, WI 54016, or his assignee ("Lender"), the principal sum of Two Hundred Fifty Thousand Dollars ($250,000.00), together with interest thereon as hereinafter provided (the "Note").

Year One Interest. The unpaid principal of this Note shall bear simple interest for 365 days from the date advanced at the rate of 100% per annum or the maximum amount of interest allowed under the laws of the State of Minnesota, whichever is less (the "Year One Interest"). On the 365th day following the date the loan is advanced, the Year One Interest shall be added to the principal balance of the loan.

Remaining Interest. From the 366th day from the date advanced until the Maturity Date set forth herein, the unpaid principal balance of this Note shall bear simple interest at the rate of 12% per annum or the maximum amount of interest allowed under the laws of the State of Minnesota, whichever is less.

Payments.

Monthly Payments. Beginning on August 15, 2022 and ending on the Maturity Date provided below, Borrower shall make payments to Lender in equal monthly installments due on the fifteenth (15th) day of each calendar month. The amount of each monthly installment payable to Lender under this section shall be Three Thousand Four Hundred Dollars ($3,400).

Maturity Date. The entire principal balance of this Note together with all accrued and unpaid interest shall be due and payable on August 11, 2026 (the "Maturity Date").

Balloon Payment at Maturity: On the Maturity Date, Borrower agrees to pay all sums that remain due under this Note, together with applicable interest, in the anticipated amount of $580,000.00

Successors. All rights, powers, privileges and immunities herein granted to Lender shall extend to its successors and assigns and any other legal holder of this Note, with full right by Lender to assign and/or sell the same.

Governing Law and Entire Agreement. This Note shall be governed by and construed in accordance with the laws of the State of Minnesota.

Signed on the day and year first above written.

TAURUS V, LLC

By: _____
Paul Thomas Croft
Its: President & CEO

DocuSigned by:

By: _____
DE2A252ABEAD438...
Pat Dougherty

11

I also received the following document from the IRA Club furthering my trust in the investment.

INVESTMENT DIRECTIONS FOR
UNSECURED LENDING

☐ NEXT BUSINESS DAY PROCESSING ($175)
Supporting documentation must be received in good order.

1. ACCOUNT OWNER INFORMATION

FULL NAME	IRA CLUB ACCOUNT NUMBER
Patrick Dougherty	1002798
LAST 4 OF SSN	PHONE NUMBER
4470	(651) 261-7174

2. BORRWER INFORMATION

BORROWER	BORROWER'S SSN/TAX ID
Taurus V, LLC	86-1741394
BORROWER'S ADDRESS	CITY, STATE, ZIP
375 Jackson St. Ste 700E	St Paul, MN 55101
BORROWER'S EMAIL ADDRESS	BORROWER'S PHONE NUMBER
paul@croftenterprisesllc.com	612-220-7692

3. LOAN INFORMATION

LOAN AMOUNT $	INTEREST RATE	MATURITY DATE
$250,000	12%	8/11/2026
TOTAL NUMBER OF PAYMENTS	PAYMENT FREQUENCY	EXPECTED PAYMENT AMOUNT
1	1	$580,000

4. NO COLLATERAL INFORMATION

By signing and submitting this form to IRA Club, you understand that the above captioned IRA account is making an unsecured loan. Unsecured loans may carry more risk than a loan back by real property or other collateral to secure repayment. IRA Club is not required to take legal action if the loan becomes default, fraud, bankrupt, or endure other legal processes. We encourage you to work with an attorney to draft, review and advise you on the terms outlined in any loan document submitted.

And now I wait!

My Pension

It's now the summer of 2022 and my retirement day is fast approaching. I was still working from home but the anticipation of life's next chapter had me in an excellent mood! Over the 50+ years I spent working there were many times it seemed like there was no end in sight but here I was, only a few months away from retirement, and I was super excited!

Late June/Early July, I was once again offered an investment opportunity but this time it involved cashing in my company pension and investing it back into ROI. I had two options for my company pension, I could take a life time annuity which paid me a guaranteed monthly income until death, or I could take a lump sum, which in my case was a roughly $365,000, to invest however I wanted. During one of several conversations during the initial investment period, the Croft & Frost Team had asked about my pension and were aware of the dynamics, so I wasn't surprised when they reached out to me with another offer for investment, but once I looked at the four scenarios they were putting on the table, I felt that the returns on all of them were unrealistic and that's when I started to get concerned with the group I was dealing with.

Here's a breakdown of what was being offered on an investment of $350K. (See original email on pages 91-93) Patrick Dougherty – One Year Return of 100%: Subsequent Years Simple Interest @ 12% for 2-5 Years

> **Option #1** – Five-Year Investment – Investment Amount $350,000, Investment Made in November 2022, $1,036,000 Total Lump Sum Payment Paid in November 2027

> **Option #2** – One Year Investment - Investment Amount $350,000, Investment Made in November 2022, $700,000 Total Lump Sum Payment Paid in November 2023

> **Option #3** – Three Year Investment – Investment Amount $350,000, 100% Interest Year One, Take Distribution of Original Investment Amount of $350,000 in 2023, 12% Simple Interest Years Two and Three, $434,000 Total Lump Sum Payment Paid in November 2025

> **Option #4** – Five Year Investment w/Monthly Payments Beginning November 2022 Investment Amount $350,000, Investment Made in November 2022, 100% Interest Year One, 12% Interest Dispersed in 48 Monthly Payments of $7000, $700,000 Total Lump Sum Payment Paid in November 2027

I had learned the value of a dollar at a young age and had always been very conservative when it came to spending and the first investment into Taurus LLC had been a really big stretch for me, so there was no way that I was going to move another $350,000 over to ROI. Plus, I had always taken a diversified approach to my 401K so I was definitely sticking to my three prong retirement plan of Social Security, Pension Payments, and Investment Draws. Never put all your eggs in one basket, right?

So I declined these offers and focused my attention on the upcoming first monthly payment from ROI and retirement on December 1st, 2022.

The Payout

My first payment was due to hit my account on August 30th, 2022, and I cannot tell you how excited I was to see the $2710 deposit when I checked online in the morning! After a year of waiting and, to be honest, worrying, I took a big sigh of relief and started dreaming about all the things I had planned in retirement. I didn't have much of a bucket list but there were a few places I had always wanted to see.

Being of Irish decent put the Emerald Island at the top of my list. Seeing the Cliffs of Moher, Kilkenny Castle, and Kissing the Blarney Stone would all be great but just sipping a Pint of Guinness while listening to authentic Celtic Music in a pub would be enough for me. And as long as I'm over there I'd like to visit the Normandy American Cemetery and Memorial in France to pay tribute to our WW2 heroes, adventure through the Alps, and check out the Nordic States because their food looks amazing! Wouldn't mind a slice of pizza with a glass of wine in Italy either.

I've always wanted to see our 49th and 50th states, Alaska and Hawaii, and seeing the country's National Parks like Yellowstone, Glacier, Yosemite, and Moab were all on my short list. But most of all I was looking forward to spending time with my kids and grandkids, and having the financial resources to maybe spoil them with family trips to Universal or Disney, nothing would give me more joy!

In the fall of 2019, I made a major purchase with retirement in mind. I'd passed that magic age of 59-1/2 and could take a withdrawal from my 401K without paying any penalties. I had found a cute little mobile home in a resort in North Western Wisconsin, a little more than an hour's drive from my primary residence. It was located in a nice resort that I was very familiar with, on one of the area's premier recreational lakes, and I already had several friends and even a few relatives located on the lake, so I contacted the seller, took a drive up, and bought the place. Then a year later I purchased a new pontoon, my first foray into the world of boating, so I was set for retirement.

My first payment of $2710 deposited on August 30th, 2022, my second payment of $2710 hit my account on September 30th, 2022, and my third payment of $2710 posted on October 30th, 2022, so I felt that I was good to go. Social Security: Check! Pension: Check! Investment Payment: Check! Lake Home w/ Pontoon: Check!

Then came November 30th, 2022, my last day of work. The next day, December 1st, I would be officially retired.

Retirement Party/First Sign of Trouble

I got up at the normal time, took a shower, made myself a cup of coffee, and logged into my computer. I was scheduled to return my work laptop at 10:00 AM and all my work accounts had already been transferred to coworkers which left me with nothing to do on my last day but bide my time, so I logged into my bank account and....... NO DEPOSIT!

I freaked out!! Where was my monthly payment? Was there an oversight somewhere? Did somebody fuck up? I needed answers but it was 6:30 AM Central Time and I knew that the IRA Club in Chicago didn't open for another two hours so at that time there was no one I could call! So, there I sat, shaking in disbelief, empty feeling in the pit of my stomach, looking at my watch every 30 seconds for the next two hours until 8:30 rolled around so I could finally contact The IRA Club to see what the hell was going on.

I got in touch with Lisa at the IRA Club. I had dealt with her on several occasions and she was very professional and very helpful. I told her that my deposit had not been made and when she looked into the situation, she told me that it was because Taurus LLC had not sent the money to The IRA Club. Per the promissory note, Taurus LLC was supposed to send the payment to the IRA Club on the 15th of every month and then they, The IRA Club, had until the 30th to process the paperwork and make my deposit. But because Taurus LLC had not held up their end of the deal there were no funds for the IRA Club to deposit into my account.

I was pissed! I fired off an email to Han Li, who was an MBA listed as the Managing Director at Golden Croft, the Investment Arm of Croft & Frost, while at the same time I sent a group text to my friends who I had invested with as they were part of the Croft & Frost Management Team working on the ROI Project. My friends replied back that they would make some phone calls and get to the bottom of what had happened but the reply from Han li was not as reassuring.

He told me that "Unfortunately" Taurus LLC did not have the funds to cover my monthly stipend but that everyone was "Working Hard" and would get the payment to me as soon as they could. I replied that this was "Unacceptable", that I was retiring "Today" and that my payment needed to be made IM-MEDIATELY! This email went unanswered.

I did get a response from my friends and they assured me that I would get my deposit the next day and told me not to worry, which at that time was easier said than done. But there was very little I could do so I decided to continue on and try to enjoy my last official day of work. I returned my laptop at 10:00, stopped by a couple of offices to say goodbye to coworkers, did a little shopping, had a late lunch, and then went to my retirement party and got lots of hugs from family, friends, and long-time coworkers. It was a great day that was overshadowed by the events that took place earlier, but that wasn't something that I wanted anyone to know so I just kept it to myself and tried as best I could to enjoy the party.

And I did!

After a very restless night of tossing and turning, I logged into my account the next morning to find not one, but two deposits of $2710! So now I'm wondering "WTF"? I emailed Han Li but got no response. I also texted my friends and they told me that they had contacted people inside the company the day before and had gotten it all worked out but weren't aware of the two payments made, so I told them that I would just consider both November and December as being paid and that we were good to go. They agreed and once again, I thought that all was good with the world!

December 30th came and went without a deposit which was expected, but then came January 2nd and there was another $2710 in my account. So again, I made a couple phone calls and it was explained away as another administrative error, so now the January 30th payment would be the "Catch up" stipend and once again we were good to go!

Or at least that's what I thought! Little did I know that this nightmare was just getting started!

Gemini Twins/Scorpio

During the year that I spent waiting for my investment payments to kick in I would often times log into Investor Meetings held by JD Frost. These were live streamed videos that would run anywhere from 30-40 minutes to over an hour in some cases, and would highlight various investment opportunities being offered by Croft & Frost. Matt Dira, who was listed as the Executive Vice President of The Dira Group, was also a visible presence at many of these meetings. His email header stated that he was a Wealth Expert and a Life and Disability Income Specialist.

In early September of 2022 I was presented with a short-term investment opportunity, Gemini Twins LLC through Matt Dira, which would pay me 20% interest over a three-month period. I had just gotten my first monthly payment a week prior and was feeling good about my investment decisions. I reached out to a couple of other investors that I knew and they told me that they had other short-term investments pay off in the past so with that confidence I went ahead and invested in Gemini Twins LLC, $35K for three months at 20% interest, maturing at $42,000 in early December of 2022.

Early December came and the Gemini Twins note came due. I was contacted by Matt Dira and given the offer to roll the now $42K over into another investment called Scorpio LLC, an investment that would once again pay 20% interest but this time over a six-month period as opposed to the previous three-month term for Gemini Twins.

Now, I'm sure you're thinking "Why, after all the confusion with his monthly payment the first of December would he reinvest with these people?", but that had been explained to me as an administrative error and I was assured that it wouldn't happen again, so I went ahead and rolled the investment over. So now I was looking at $42,000 at 20% for six months, paying out $50,400 in early June of 2023. Another promissory note was sent via DocuSign, and the deal was done.

Both the Scorpio and Gemini Twins Promissory Notes were signed by JD Frost and below is a confirmation document sent to me on 12/15/22, outlining the terms of the agreement. Please note that the address on the document header is 1413 Chestnut Street, Chattanooga TN, 37402, which at the time was the physical address of Croft & Frost Accounting. The $10M building recently went into foreclosure and was purchased for less than half its value and I will have more on that later.

SCORPIO

1413 Chestnut St #401, Chattanooga, TN 37402, United States

Investor Information:		Account Statement Period: 10/1/22-12/31/22	
Name:	Pat Dougherty	For:	Q4 2022
		Due:	1/31/2023

Date	Description	Maturity Date	Interest Rate	Invested	Period Interest Earned
12/15/22	20% 6 Months	6/15/23	25%	$42,000.00	N/A

Total: $42,000.00

Thank you for your business!

Should you have any enquiries concerning this statement, please contact Matt Dira on (804) 920-2463

Arizona

At the end of January, 2023, I took a 10-day trip to Arizona to visit my older sister and her husband, they are retired and have a winter home in Gold Canyon which is Southeast of Phoenix. The morning of February first I went online to check my account to make sure that my pension check had been deposited and also to transfer that overpayment from January into my checking. Everything looked good.

I decided to call Lisa at The IRA Club just to double check that we were back on track with the monthly payments and it was then that she informed me that my account was now showing a negative $3400 balance, so basically, I was now in the red. Once again, I freaked out!! I asked how that could be, as I thought that all the confusion over the double payments had been resolved and things were back on track.

She informed me that the account was originally set up to auto pay every month on the 30th but that was predicated on Taurus LLC meeting their commitment of transferring the funds on the 15th of the month as required by the promissory agreement. Apparently, there had not been a funds transfer from Taurus since that early December deposit which squared the account, that meant that the early January auto payment put me into a negative balance. When I asked about the double payment in early December, she knew nothing about it! WTF??

OK, Now I'm confused!!

Since my sister started wintering in Arizona, I had made several trips down to stay with them and had always spent the entire time in the Phoenix area. This time, I had a three-day road trip planned that would have me spending two days in Sedona and another day at the Grand Canyon, two places that I had always wanted to visit. Obviously, I had a serious problem that I had to deal with regarding my investment in ROI, but at that moment my personal account was square and considering that it was all out of my hands at that time I decided to carry on with my vacation plans and enjoy my time in Arizona. My sister and her husband have a beautiful home in a gated golf community and are gracious hosts who always make my stay there enjoyable. And all I can say about Sedona and the Grand Canyon is WOW!! Definitely going back to that part of the country again!

I did make a call to my friends who work at Croft & Frost and vented my continued frustrations with them and, once again, they assured me that they would talk to JD and get to the bottom of what was going on.

Delays, Runarounds, Frustrations

I've always been someone who saves and documents things, especially when it comes to finances. When I moved from the house my kids grew up in to the townhome where I now reside, I was throwing out paid receipts for electric, gas, mortgage, etc that were 10-15 years old. I think it's a Baby Boomer thing!

I had been keeping general documentation pertaining to my investments with Taurus LLC, Gemini Twins LLC, and Scorpio LLC, but it was becoming clear that that I had also better start documenting all my communications with Croft & Frost and related entities as well, just in case these ongoing issues did not get resolved and I needed to take legal action.

From this point, as I continue sharing my story, I will provide direct text conversations from the dozens of communications I had with employees of Croft & Frost, but specifically, the many text messages with JD Frost, because I feel they are the best way for me to tell my story to you. These conversations explicitly show the level of deception and lies that JD Frost utilized to keep me strung along in what I now believed was an illegal Ponzi Scheme. I will also provide screenshots of the actual texts as references in the back of the book.

Start of the Dance

February 15th, 2023, the due date for my February payment to be wired from Taurus LLC to the IRA Club. Although the provisions of the promissory note stated that Taurus LLC was to transfer funds to the IRA Club on the 15th of every month it also gave them a 10-day grace period meaning the payment was actually due on the 25th of each month, and if it was not received by the IRA Club by the 25th there would be a penalty of 2% added to the initial payment.

Knowing that the 25th was the "real" due date for the funds transfer I waited until February 21st before reaching out to Lisa at the IRA Club. After a minute or two she confirmed that there had been not transfer of funds from Taurus LLC which gave me yet another sick feeling in the pit of my stomach. After bemoaning the situation, I thanked her for her time and set my sights on another go around with the contacts at Croft & Frost.

I put in a call to Han Li, Managing Director at Croft & Frost, but got his voice mail so I left him a long message conveying my heightened level of frustration to him. Within a few minutes I received the text message below and I am including my response for reference.

Received from Han Li on 2/21/23 at 9:44 AM (See original texts on pages 94& 95)

> **Han Li:** Hi Pat, this is Han. I'm not able to get on the phone right now, but your payment was sent

out this morning. So, you will receive it soon once it's processed through the IRA Club.

My Response: I appreciate the update, Han, but per our agreement these payments are to be made on the 15th of the month and not the 21st as has been done this month. As I stated in my VM I am dependent on this investment to pay my bills in retirement and cannot have any reservations on whether or not these payments are going to be made, so moving forward I don't know what needs to be done to ensure the payments are on time every month but something needs to be done to ensure that they are transmitted on the 15th as agreed upon by Taurus LLC and myself. We have 41 months to go and the fact that we've had so many issues in the first six months does not give me a sense of security on this!

Received from Han Li on 2/21/23 at 9:59 AM

HL: I understand your concerns and this is temporary as we are working on getting our ROI project fully funded. These delays will be resolved very soon going forward.

The funds were received by the IRA Club that day and I got my deposit on the 28th as schedule, so once again I could pay my bills and stay afloat, but it was becoming very clear that there was a problem, a big problem, and my confidence that this situation was going to get resolved was quickly eroding!

I would like to point out that in Han's last text he states that my payments are tied to getting the ROI Project fully funded. This is the first time that I was told by anyone at Croft & Frost that my monthly payments were directly dependent on funding from another source. It was never brought up in the June, 2021, conference call, it's not listed in the promissory note, and it's nowhere to be found in any of the paperwork that I received from Croft & Frost, Taurus LLC, or The IRA Club. Had this little bit of information been given to me from the start I would never have invested in ROI, but apparently that was by design!

The Email

February 25th, I had gotten to a breaking point and decided it was time to reach out to everyone involved and get a few things off my chest!

It was early on a Saturday when I sat down at my computer with a fresh cup of coffee straight from my Keurig, and I proceeded to type an email outlining my frustrations with the ongoing issues regarding my ROI Investment and Croft & Frost. Paul Croft was listed as the President of not only Croft & Frost but also ROI, and because it was his signature on the promissory note, I addressed it directly to him and Cc'd everyone at Croft & Frost and The IRA Club who I had addresses for.

The email is much too long and detailed to post here so here's the highlights to give you some context.

I started by reminding Paul of the parameters laid out in the promissory note/agreement that he had signed. That was followed by a full description, in painstaking detail, of everything I had experienced over the previous six months, from the late payments, to the double payments, to the general runaround I felt I was getting from Croft & Frost. I reiterated that I was retired and dependent on him to meet his obligations so that I, in turn, could meet mine. And, finally, I asked him to please advise on how these issues were going to be resolved so that there would be no more delays moving forward.

Within minutes, Paul fired a reply back, copying everyone on the original email chain, stating sternly "At Croft & Frost we pay our bills"!!! That was it, his entire reply!

Then, a couple minutes later, I get another reply from JD, this one addressed only to me, that simply said "Pat, here's my number, please give me a call and let's talk, JD."

When I considered the combination of a bad night's sleep, several cups of coffee, my pent-up frustration, and my elevated blood pressure from seeing Paul's reply, I decided it would be wise to wait until I calmed down before calling, so after lunch I got on the phone with JD Frost.

He was at a volleyball game or tournament with one of his daughters, and when I told him that my daughter had also played volleyball when she was younger that led to a brief conversation about family and kids. I always found JD to be a nice, friendly, person and easy to talk to. He comes across as genuinely likable.

The conversation then turned to the business at hand. He told me that Paul was the President of the company and that, even though his signature was on my promissory note, he really didn't have much to do with the day-to-day operations of Croft & Frost. That's when he told me to come directly to him with any and all issues and he would handle them for me, basically being my go-to guy from here on out.

I said "Okay" and thanked him for being proactive with regards to my situation. We hung up on good terms and I actually felt better about things. Unfortunately, those good feelings were not going to last for long!

Winter at the Lake

In March I headed to South Padre Island for some much-needed sun and sand. I was meeting up with high school friends who were all either retired or semi-retired, and the goal was to just relax and have a good time. While it was great spending time with my friends the trip was not as relaxing as I had hope for. It was spring break so the island was swamped with college kids which made it really hard to go anywhere for dinner or drinks. It was also one of the coldest spring breaks SPI had seen in years so that basically killed the whole "sun and sand" concept.

As it usually goes, the sun finally made an appearance on my last day there and the temps rose to near 90, so I threw on my swim trunks and headed to the pool to soak up as much Vitamin D as possible before heading home the next morning.

I was sitting poolside, enjoying the warmth while sipping a Strawberry Daiquiri, and my phone rang. It was Kirk, one of the owners of the resort where my cabin is located. The Wisconsin winter of 2022-2023 had seen record snowfalls and he was calling to inform me that the roof on my cabin had collapsed. He didn't know how much damage had been done but he did send me a few pictures he took from the outside and also through the windows and it didn't look good.

I forwarded the pictures on to my kids and a few close friends, posted them on Facebook, and of course, notified my insurance agent. After stewing on it for a few minutes I realized that there was nothing I could do in that moment so I shrugged my shoulders and went back to the sunshine and Strawberry Daiquiris, and I needed a lot of them to forget the troubles that were waiting for me 1600 miles away in Northern Wisconsin.

Luckily, there was no delay in the March payment from Croft & Frost so that's one headache I was able to avoid when I got home.

The Real Trouble Begins!

4/20, a National Holiday for Pot Smokers and I was at the point where I needed a joint the size of a baseball bat!

The adjuster had been to my cabin and declared it a total loss, so I was in the process of itemizing the contents so that the insurance company could come up with a fair amount to pay off on the loss.

As I looked at the damage, I knew that replacing the mobile home was going to be an expensive process, and considering that my retirement budget was already tight, I couldn't deal with anymore disruptions with my monthly payouts from Croft & Frost. On the morning of 4/20/23 I sent a text to both Han Li and JD Frost, reminding them of the April payment date. Below is that texting exchange.

Sent to JD Frost and Han Li on 4/20/23 at 8:53 AM (See original text on page 96)

> **ME:** Good morning, Han, hope you are well. Pat Dougherty here with a friendly reminder that it's the 20th of the month so please make sure my monthly payment is made to the IRA Club today, thanks!

JD replied at 10:33 AM

JD: Hey, Pat, we should have that ready at the latest next Friday.

Me: Next Friday is the 27th and my deposit from the IRA Club is made on the 28th so that's not going to work, can it be made by next Mondy the 24th?

JD: We will do our best.

Payment was not received by The IRA Club on the 27th so I called JD and left him a very direct voicemail message venting my frustration and asking what the holdup was, below is his reply via text message.

Received from JD on 5/1/23 at 10:05 AM. (See original text on Page 97)

JD: This is from the IRA Club – Pat's disbursement going out today, it is set as ACH so he will get tomorrow.

Me: As we discussed last Friday the promissory note states a grace of 10 days and after that the borrower pays the lender a 2% late fee so that's an extra $68.00, will that be included?

JD: We are sending to the IRA Club today. Yes Sir.

5/1/23 at 4:42 PM

JD: Your payment was released today with the penalty amount.

JD: Should be there today or tomorrow.

JD: Thank you for your patience.

Received from JD Frost on 5/2/23 at 8:24 AM (See original text on page 98)

JD: Good morning, Pat. I wanted to check and make sure that payment went through for you.

Me: Hasn't been deposited yet so you may want to check with the IRA Club.

JD: OK, cool, we sent it so it should show today. Thank you and hope you have a great day.

Sent to JD the next morning, 5/3/23 at 9:07 AM (See original text on page 98)

ME: Still no payment received by the IRA Club! If this isn't taken care of by this afternoon, I will be seeking legal counsel! This is BULLSHIT!

JD replied at 9:35 AM

JD: I believe we have the issue figured out. We are sending the IRA today, this morning.

Sent from JD on 5/3/23 at 10:25 AM (See original text on pages 99 & 100)

JD: Since it was a little different amount because of the late fee added on there it was not sent to your account. We are confirming with the IRA Club now but that is our suspicion.

Me: Ok, please keep me posted.

JD: Did you get Venmo set up?

Please note the gap in texting from 4/20/23 and 5/3/23. During this time, I was engaging with JD on the phone, continuing to express my frustration with the entire investment situation. I had told him about my cabin, about the need to purchase a new mobile home to replace the one that was completely lost in the collapse, and not only did I tell him that I could not handle any more delays in my monthly payments (Yeah, I know, starting to sound like a broken record, right?), I also notified him that I would be cashing the Scorpio LLC Note for $50,400 that was due on June 15th because I needed that money to offset the difference that insurance was not covering. He acknowledged my request to cash in on Scorpio.

He also offered to send me $3400 out of his own pocket for the purpose of acting as a "buffer" just in case he couldn't get a regular Taurus payment to me on time. I remember pausing on the phone before saying "Are you fucking kidding me"? I asked why, if he had the $3400, couldn't he just send it to The IRA Club as my payment so that they could take the taxes and make my deposit keeping everything above board, and his response was that it would be too complicated.

At the time I did not have the Venmo app on my phone so he advised me to download it. I told him that I would not accept his money if it, in any way, interfered with his obligation of paying my normal monthly stipend and he assured me that it wouldn't. He said that it would only be a good faith gesture, by him, to give me a "cushion" just in case he was late one month with a payment. So, after much self-debate, I downloaded Venmo and accepted JD's offer of $3400 in cash.

In the following text string between myself and JD you will see that he was late, once again, on the normally scheduled payment, he continues to make a variety of excuses as to why the payment is late, and he is also working to get me the $3400 in a Venmo transfer. The texts start on 5/8/23 and carry on until 5/15/23, when he makes a final payment of $1000 via Venmo.

And on a side note, he told me that Venmo had a daily limit that wouldn't allow him to send the full $3400 at one time, and that's not true. Once your account has been established you can send up to $5000 per day, but I ended up getting four separate Venmo payments, $505, $1000, $1000, and $895, so I can only assume this was because he was also doing this with other investors! Unbelievable!

Sent to JD on 5/8/23 at 7:31 AM (See original text on page 101)

> **Me:** Good morning JD, just sent you an email so please see and reply ASAP, thanks!

> **JD:** Great, Thank you.

Sent to JD on 5/9/23 at 12:47 PM (See original texts on pages 101-103)

> **Me:** Did you get that $3400 sent over to the IRA Club yet?

> **JD:** Not yet

Me: Do you have a timeframe on that?

JD: Venmo is easier to make happen fast

JD: But probably end of the week at worst

5/9/23 at 1:02 PM

Me: So, if we do Venmo directly to me that will not affect the May payment due later this month, correct? This one-time Venmo is designed to be a buffer, correct?

JD: Yes

JD: Exactly

JD: Meant to be peace of mind

Me: And I will still get my scheduled May payment due by the end of the month?

JD: Yes

Me: OK, so what do you need to know about my Venmo account to send me the money?

JD: What's your Venmo name?

Me: Would that be my username?

JD: Yes

Me: (Provided Venmo Username)

Me: Does that look right?

JD: Yes!!!

Me: OK, does Venmo give me a notice when the money is deposited?

JD: (Thumbs Up)

Me: OK, let me know when you send it

Sent to JD on 5/10/23 at 9:40 AM (See original texts on pages 104-106)

Me: That $505 was received from Venmo and successfully deposited into my bank account so go ahead and send me the remaining $2895

JD: Will do if it lets me send

Sent on 5/11/23 at 8:38 AM

Me: On a different note, are you going to send the remaining $2985 to my Venmo?

JD: Just tried sending another $1000 and it did not go through. Sometimes Venmo limits you on the amount you can send on a weekly basis. We will get it done

JD: Just sent another $1000

Me: I was reading all the rules and regs on the Venmo site and it states that individual payments up to $5000 can be made so something doesn't add up on that. Please keep trying and let me know when it goes through

Sent to JD on 5/15/23

Me: That $1000 just hit my account, thanks!

Received from JD on 5/18/23

JD: No problem

JD: Thanks for your trust

The Walls Start to Close In

In early June I attended a graduation party for the daughter of some good friends who I had worked with for many years. I rode to that party with my friends who were working for Paul and JD, the ones who had brought me on as an Investor in the ROI Project.

It was a beautiful summer day, perfect for an outdoor grad party, and I had a great time visiting with many former coworkers who I hadn't seen since retiring seven months earlier. At about 7:30-8:00 we said our goodbyes and headed back to my friend's house. He was driving, she was in the front passenger seat, and I was sitting in the middle of the back seat of their car.

Our conversation was what I would call normal. We were recapping the party and talking about who we had seen, how good the food was, etc… and about half way home my friend says that she needs to tell me something. I'm like "Okay."

Suddenly, she becomes very animated and tells me that they, the two of them, have not been paid by Croft & Frost for something like three months, and she just unleashes a profanity laced diatribe on Paul and JD, mostly on JD, and in this rant she's throwing out words like "Fraud" and "Ponzi" and I'm sitting in the backseat, speechless, feeling my heart about to pound right out of my chest! I'd be lying if I said that, after what I had experienced the previous six months, any of this surprised me, but hearing it come from these two confirmed the worst of my fears!

I was screwed!

When we got back to their place, we opened up a bottle of wine and spent an hour or so discussing the situation. They were going to continue working with the hopes that things would turnaround, which would obviously be beneficial to me, and I agreed not to mention to JD that I knew about the nonpayment of salaries. After saying my goodbyes, I went home to what I would describe as one of the most restless nights of my entire life, it was horrible!

The next day I assessed my situation. My cabin at the lake was completely destroyed and it was going to cost me $6500 to have it demolished and hauled away. Replacing it with a new mobile home was going to cost three times more than the original one meaning that instead of having a cabin that was 100% paid for I was now going to be taking on debt, something that I had not budgeted for when I made my decision to retire. A big chunk of my retirement savings are tired up in two investments, one for $250,000 that is supposed to be paying out a $3400 monthly stipend that I have to poke and prod to get every month, and another for $50,400 that was schedule to pay out in another week, and now I find out that the company I'm invested with is three months behind on salaries for their employees! Yeah, things weren't looking too good at that point!

Time to go on Offense

They say that Knowledge is Power, and now that I knew about the situation at Croft & Frost I felt I had a little more power to guide the conversation into the direction that I needed it to go. Of the two investment issues, I felt the most pressing was Scorpio because #1, that was due to pay out on June 15th and #2, I needed that money to pay for the things I was dealing with at the lake.

I decided that my best approach would be to change the tone of my interactions with JD and start being more friendly with him. One of the first things I picked up when speaking to him was his narcissistic arrogance, it was easy to tell that nobody loved JD more than JD loved JD, so I lowered the temperature of my emails, my texts, and my phone calls because he held the keys to getting my $50,400 back, and that would determine whether I would or wouldn't have a lake home.

From the moment I found out about my cabin collapsing I had been in JD's ear so he was well aware of what I was going through, and once June rolled around, I called him multiple times to reiterate the need to get the Scorpio Note cashed and the funds transferred to The IRA Club for distribution.

Now I am working him on two different fronts. There's the ongoing push to get my monthly payment and the urgent need for JD to meet the June 15th deadline on cashing out the Scorpio Note. My stress level was running very high, or as Nigel Tufnel from Spinal Tap would say, it was turned up to 11! But I had to keep cool because there was too much on the line and JD held all the cards and I desperately need to win a hand!

The following interactions with JD are over a one-month period, starting on 6/7/23, and ending on 7/5/23. They show JD's continued efforts to avoid making his required payments to me.

Sent to JD on 6/7/23 at 11:14 AM (See original text on page 106)

> **Me:** I need to know that my Scorpio note is going to cash out next week so please advise ASAP!
>
> **JD:** At this point in time, we are working on making sure that happens
>
> **Me:** Okay, keep me posted
>
> **JD:** Yes sir

Sent to JD on 6/20/23 at 7:45 AM (See original text on page 107)

> **Me:** Good morning JD, just a reminder that today is the 20th so please be sure to get my monthly payment sent to the IRA Club ASAP. As I stated before I need the funds deposited by the first of the month so that means the funds need to be sent by the 27th of the month. Please confirm, thanks!
>
> **JD:** Yes, we are sending the payment
>
> **JD:** We are on track as of right now to meet the deadline on the 27th

Me: OK, thanks!

Sent to JD on 6/21/23 at 9:34 AM (See original text on page 108)

> **Me:** Hi, JD, did the funds get sent yesterday as you stated?
>
> **JD:** Yes, the Taurus monthly payment did
>
> **Me:** Okay, thanks!
>
> **Me:** And we're still looking good on Scorpio cashout withing the next 2-3 weeks?
>
> **JD:** Yes sir

At this point my stress level was building and I continued to text JD reminding him that the Scorpio Note was due!

Sent to JD on 7/5/23 at 10:04 AM (See original text on page 109)

> **Me:** Good morning, JD, and Happy Friday! We are now 15 days into the 30-day grace period for the payoff of the Scorpio note so please confirm that we are still on target and provide the actual date if possible
>
> **JD:** We are still on target. As long as everything goes to planned, we are looking at end of next week

Me: Okay

I reached out to JD after the 4th of July to apply a little pressure, he needed to get those Scorpio funds transferred to The IRA Club ASAP!

Sent to JD on 6/30/23 at 12:05 PM (See original texts on pages 110-111)

> **Me:** Please confirm that the funds for the Scorpio note will be sent to the IRA Club by the end of the week as you said they would. I'm only a couple weeks out from getting my new place delivered to the lake and desperately need those funds! Thanks!

> **JD:** Good Morning

> **Me:** Good afternoon now

> **JD:** This is set to be sent to the IRA Club today

> **JD:** I am still in Hawaii; we get back Friday to Chattanooga

Didn't think about it at the time but once the shit hit the fan, I realized that he was vacationing in Hawaii, with his wife and kids, using my money!

I Continued to press him!

> **Me:** $50,400 going to my IRA Club account today?

JD: Yes sir

Me: Great! I will follow up with Lisa then and thank you for your attention to this. I wish you and your family safe travels back to TN

JD: Thank you, buddy

YES!!!
Received from JD on 7/5/23 at 2:10 PM (See original text on page 112)

JD: Payment Confirmed

JD: Should be there later today or tomorrow

Me: You're the best!

JD: Thank you. Working really hard to earn your trust back, Pat

Me: And that work is greatly appreciated!

On July 5th, 2023, after badgering JD for several months, he transferred $50,400 to my account at The IRA Club and I had it immediately transferred into another IRA account with Cetera, one "small" problem taken care of and now it was onto the bigger issue at hand, how was I going to get my $250,000 back from the Taurus Fund? Was that even possible? I wasn't giving up hope, not yet, but I read the tea leaves and things did not look promising!

July, August, and September

July and August brought more of the same. I continued to send JD texts pertaining to my monthly payments, and he in turn continued to make excuses for why he couldn't meet the scheduled deadlines.

The text string below starts on 7/20/23 and runs through 7/27/23, they contain the normal JD spin, nothing new to see here. But if you look closely, you may see something that's not present in any of his other text replies, maybe you'll catch it but if you don't I'll be sure to point it out to you.

Sent to JD on 7/20/23 not time stamped (See original text on page 113)

> **Me:** Good morning, JD, I hope this text finds you well. Just the monthly reminder that it's the 20th so please make sure that my Taurus payment is sent to the IRA Club in time to make the scheduled direct deposit on the 28th, thanks!
>
> **Me:** Enjoy your day!
>
> **JD:** Good Morning
>
> **JD:** We are receiving payments next week for our investments as they are not still quite on track

so will be able to make that payment by end of next week

Me: So, it will be sent to the IRA Club by Friday next week, the 28th?

JD: Yes sir

Me: OK, I will check in mid-week just to be sure, thanks again

JD: Yes, that would be great. Thanks for the follow up

Sent to JD on 7/25/23 at 8:08 AM (See original text on pages 114-115)

Me: Hi, JD, I need my Taurus payment deposited into my account by Friday so please confirm that it will be sent to the IRA Club today, thanks!

JD: It will not be sent today. We will send on Thursday this week. This is the reason I sent the extra $3400 to you for times like this

Me: OK, Thursday will work, thanks!

Sent to JD on 7/27/23 at 8:18 AM

Me: Good morning, please confirm that the payment will be sent to the IRA Club today, thanks!

JD: We will confirm when sent

7/25/23 at 3:06 PM

Me: Please confirm payment has been sent

JD: Have not sent today, we are awaiting funds

Me: So, when will it be sent?

JD: At this moment will be by Wednesday next week

And BOOM, there it is!! Did you see it?

Look closely at the 3rd to the last line, JD states that he is "awaiting funds" so that he can make a payment to me!

According to the Legal Information Institute at Cornell University, the definition of a Ponzi Scheme is a type of investment fraud in which investors are promised artificially high rates of return with little or no risk. Original investors and the perpetrators of the fraud are paid off by funds of later investors, but there is little to no actual business activity that produces revenue.

It never dawned on me at the time, only in retrospect did I realize what that one line in that one text signified! Makes me feel like such a chump now!

My new cabin was being delivered in a few days and the financial stresses were mounting. I needed JD to get his shit together and start living up to his commitments and stop dicking around, so I stayed after him!

The text conversation continues.

7/25/23 at 4:59 PM (See original texts on pages 116-117)

Me: That's not good

JD: I know, had some hang ups with a payment but should be good to go next week

Me: Okay

Sent to JD on 7/31/23 at 8:05 AM

Me: Need my Payment, JD, so please confirm that it will be sent tomorrow as promised in our last text

JD: Yes, understand that we are getting our payment today and will release as soon as possible today. Thank you for your patience

Me: My new trailer is being delivered to the lake tomorrow and I will be writing an $85K check so it absolutely has to be in my account by Friday, no exceptions!

JD: That's awesome

JD: Pat, I am not creating expectations

Me: I am about to take on additional debt of roughly $70K and am looking at a monthly payment of close to $1K which was not budgeted for when I retired so now, in order to keep my cabin at the lake, I have to rely on my investment with you consistently paying out by the first of every month, otherwise my place at the lake will be gone!

Me: You have a lake home so you understand the value they bring to our family and friends

JD: Gives a "thumbs up" and "likes" my comment

JD: Yes, of course

JD: And we will make it happen for you

Notice that one of JD's replies is a "Like" of my rant stating that if he doesn't get his shit together, I will lose my lake home! What an idiot!

Of, course, payment still took another week to hit my account.

Read on.

Sent to JD on 8/2/23 at 8:04 (See original text on pages 118-119)

Me: Good morning, just checking in on my payment, will it be sent to the IRA Club today?

JD: Yes

Sent to JD on 8/3/23 at 8:51

Me: No payment was sent to the IRA Club yesterday, are you going to meet your obligations or not?

JD: We had to send it today, it's a long story

JD: Yes, we are going to meet our obligations

JD: Do you still have that extra $3400 I sent you personally?

Me: Yes, but when you sent me that we agreed it would not change the structure of the monthly payments. It's not that I can't meet my obligations because I do pull off that $3400 and then replenish it when I get my actual payment but the continued struggle with getting this done on time is extremely frustrating and we have to find a solution.

Me: I'm off to the lake so I'll be offline, please make sure that goes today

JD: Doing everything we can to ensure it goes today

Sent at 4:54 PM later that day

Me: Did it get sent? **JD:** Yes sir

July was a very stressful month for me. On one hand, I was applying full court pressure on JD to get him to pay the $50,400 on the Scorpio note while at the same time continuing to push him on getting my monthly annuity payments sent to the IRA Club so I could pay my bills. Both were crucial in getting my new cabin set up.

JD held all the cards but, because I had been told about the turmoil inside of ROI back in June, I felt that I had a little bit of a leg up on him, so I continued to be cordial and cooperative, even complimentary at times, in order to keep the money flowing. JD had control of a large chunk of my life savings, and I still held out hope of getting my money back!

I tend to be a pretty even keeled person, and it takes a lot to get me mad. Early in August it was brought to my attention that in July, during the time that I was texting JD, working to get my payment sent and having him give me excuse after excuse for why the payment hadn't been sent, JD was sending those texts from a golf course in Scotland.

Yep, that's right! While I'm stressing out here in Wisconsin, dealing with demolition costs, concrete foundation costs, plumbing, gas, and HVAC contracting costs, JD was on a once in a lifetime golfing vacation in Scotland spending my money! Family vacation to Hawaii in June, golfing vacation to Scotland in July! Must have been nice!

Is it Douchebag or Douche Bag? Asshole or Ass Hole?

I had to stay on JD all through August and I finally got my payment scheduled for the 28th on September 3rd. And just for the record, that 2% late fee that I was supposed to be getting I never got. It should have been $68 added to the $3400 but when JD can't manage to make the schedule payments how can I have any expectations that he would follow through on the late fees?

It was Friday afternoon, September 8th, and I was driving to the cabin. My phone rang and I could see on the hands-free screen that it was JD. Earlier that day I had been given a heads up by my friends that the entire management staff at ROI had walked out and resigned and I was sure that JD's call was nothing more than a fishing expedition because he knew that I was friends with some of the newly resigned managers.

I took his call, we had some small talk, he asked me about the new cabin, if I was "happy" with everything, thanked me for my continued "trust" in him, and promised that he would continue working very hard to make ROI a great success. All this BS had me rolling my eyes because I already knew that ROI was in a lot of trouble and I also knew that meant JD was in deep shit too! But I played along, what else could I do?

We ended our call with a cordial "Talk to you later" and that was it, that was the last time I spoke to JD Frost.

On September 12th the accounting firm of Croft & Frost shut their doors, leaving dozens of employees without work and countless customers scrambling at, what apparently, is tax time for some. It was soon revealed that the Croft & Frost employees had also gone months without being paid, and according to news reports when they were paid it was money that came out of other funds like those related to ROI. Paul and JD had been playing the ultimate shell game, but instead of a peanut, it was people's livelihoods they were playing with and they couldn't have cared less!

On 9/14/23 I sent the following text message to JD at 3:23 PM (See original text on page 120)

> **Me:** So, is my investment secure or am I shit out of luck?
>
> **JD:** I'm seeking council this week, will have better answers soon
>
> **Me:** Okay, well please keep me posted because I believed in you and I sure hope you don't let me down
>
> **JD:** I know you do and I appreciate that

Sent to JD on 9/18/23 at 9:16 AM (See original text on page 120)

> **Me:** Good morning JD, hope you were able to enjoy some of your weekend. It's the 18th and I need to know if you're going to be able to make the monthly payment by the first of October and please be honest with me, thanks.

He did not respond.

Sent to JD on 9/18/23 at 6:08 PM (See original text on page 120)

> **Me:** Just drove two hours to get to my cabin. I need to know if you are going to meet your obligation and get me my monthly payment or if you're not. The only way I can keep this place is if I get my interest payments on a regular monthly basis

Once again, he did not respond.

And that was it, that was the last communications I had with JD Frost. I found out the next day that both Paul and JD had taken down all of their social media pages, which for those two narcists was a telling sign, and neither was answering calls or texts. For lack of a better term, they went dark!

The Fallout and More Scamming

Friday, September 15th, three days after Croft & Frost had closed their doors, an email was sent to a group of over 250 investors, it was from Paul Croft. He wanted to assure us that our investments were safe from the issues with Croft & Frost and wouldn't be affected by the reported closing.

Received from Paul on 9/15/23 at 4:52 PM (See original email on page 124)

> I'm Paul Croft, majority shareholder of ROI.
>
> There have been a lot of conversations surrounding the closing of our accounting firm, Croft & Frost. I want to be the first to tell you that ROI and the investment subsidiaries are separate entities from Croft & Frost.
>
> We continue our diligent work to get this deal closed for all our investors. We have also enlisted the help of a few of the major investors to help get this deal across the finish line.
>
> We are meeting as a group this weekend and will set up calls next week to inform our investors on status. My apologies for any concerns the closing

of Croft & Frost have caused. We have reason to be confident that the deal will get done.

ONWARD - Paul T Croft

I wasn't sure how everyone else felt but I knew this was all Bullshit!

Trying to Cover my Ass

Throughout the summer I realized that things were getting worse so I started to badger JD for some sort of statement of account, telling him that I wanted to see how my money was working for me. In reality, I felt that the writing was on the wall and I was trying to get as much documentation as possible, knowing that I may need it down the road. I am providing screenshots of my email, his response, and the report that was provided. (See original email and report on pages 121-123).

Please note that the date on the email is August 29th, 2023. This was exactly two weeks before the closing of Croft & Frost and the discontinuation of my monthly annuity payments, so I can only assume that these numbers were just pulled out of thin air as JD had to have known that the ROI investments were already gone. This is just another example of the depths of deception he was willing to go through to keep his scheme going.

Learning the Size and Scope/ Banding Together

W ithin a few days I received notice of an upcoming zoom call for investors and Paul was not included in the copy list. The purpose of the meeting was to discuss options for getting our investments back, and the possibility of banding together to file a class action suit. The zoom call was attended by several of the recently resigned ROI Team who, one by one, introduced themselves and took the rath of multiple participants in the meeting.

I just sat and listened.

In the meeting I heard several heartbreaking stories of loss. One woman had served in the military and upon retirement had cashed out her pension and moved it into another type of savings' fund. JD had persuaded her to invest the entire sum into ROI, so after decades of service to her country they left her with nothing!

Another investor, a young man I would estimate to be in his mid-30s, had worked as an accountant for Croft & Frost and had also invested heavily in ROI, so not only did he go months without a paycheck, he also lost his job and all of his savings. And to make things worse, he had three young children at home and his wife was going through chemo and he wasn't sure if he was even going to be able to make the mortgage payments to keep the roof over his family's heads!

And then there was the story of the Investors who had tragically lost their son and had to experience, as they put it, "The

Shame" of having their friends put together a Go Fund Me page just to cover the funeral expenses, and that's due exclusively to the fact that they lost their life's savings investing with Paul and JD!

He was 25 years old and his name was Eli.

JD owned a building in Downtown Chattanooga and it recently went into foreclosure. It's been reported that the building had an estimated value of $10M and, apparently, his wealthy family stepped in and bought it for $5.8M. Someone doesn't have to be good at math to see that as a net profit $4.2M for the Frost family. I'm not implying that there was anything wrong with the transaction because I understand that business is business, but I do find it sad that a family who prides itself on its philanthropy would seek to profit off a situation that has negatively affected so many lives! A donation to help with Eli's funeral expenses would have been nice!

1 Corinthians 15:33 "Bad Company Ruins Good Morals."

Moving on.

Within a few hours of the zoom meeting Paul responded. He had either listened in on the call or had someone listening for him because he knew everything that was said, and once again he said that everything was fine, that the former ROI Management Team was lying, and that as President of the company he hadn't been involved with the day-to-day operations like he should have been but moving forward he would make sure to be more hands on!

Over the next few weeks we had 3-4 more zoom meetings, I scanned all my documentation into a file and sent it on to someone, someplace, and from what I know there's an active class action suit that's been filed in Chicago but by all indications it looks like these two blew through all the money, so I truly doubt that I'll ever get any portion of my investment back!

I don't know the exact dollar amount but I've been told that it's somewhere in the $40M-$50M range, so I sure hope those two clowns had a good time because they left a lot of damage in their wake!

Paul Continues to Lie, I Start to Troll

One thing about narcissists, they're just not smart enough to know when to shut up!

A month after the closing of Croft & Frost, the Investor Group started receiving weekly emails containing an attached "Update" from Paul. By this time, there were multiple civil suits filed against the two of them, claiming fraud, for amounts in the hundreds of thousands of dollars, so I'm not sure what Paul thought he had to gain by sending these emails out but they were definitely falling flat with the Investors.

I looked at the updates as nothing more than Paul's attempts at continuing the scam, and at that point I was more than fed up with his bullshit and decided to sarcastically respond. Below are the email updates Paul sent over a six week span, from Mid-October, 2023, to Early December, 2023, along with my replies. You can see that as Paul's updates got more and more ridiculous, and my responses got more and more sarcastic.

In all cases I copied the entire Investors Group.

Received from Paul on 10/13/23 (See original email on pages 124-125)

Dear investors of ROI

Please accept his letter as my continued effort to be transparent with you regarding the latest with ROI.

One, I do not have the financials for ROI yet. I continue to seek these so we can all understand the current state of the investments.

Two, as some of you already know and with no intent to be braggadocious, my skill set is best utilized in forging connections amongst people, sharing a vision that is mutually beneficial, inspiring others to believe in that vision, and working tenaciously to achieve that vision by placing people in the right position. To that end, I am the first to say I am not qualified to manage the production of a hydrogen facility plant. The breadth and scope of the technology involved is beyond my education. This is why ROI had a management team in place and needs new day in, day out, operators to carry this company forward. In addition, I am the first to say I am not qualified to handle the bookkeeping and accounting for a company such as ROI.

I have been back with the company for 30 days now. Over the last weeks, I have stepped into what I do best by attempting to secure investments and/or financing to help ROI secure new, more competent management to get the aforementioned fully executed funding contracts to fruition. There are some interested investors but until I have a legal agreement fully executed, I cannot claim it's been achieved. In football terms, I believe we're approaching the red zone. What I do best will certainly be a key component for ROI to keep moving forward. I hope to deliver some good news on this front in the upcoming weeks.

Sincerely
Paul Croft

The next day I sent the following sarcastic reply to Paul and copied the Investors Group:

Paul,

While you're working on "doing what you do best" I'm in the process of selling my lake home because you have defaulted on your commitment to pay me a monthly interest stipend on my investment, so instead of these late Friday afternoon letters that tell us absolutely nothing please explain to us where all of the money we invested has gone and why a person who claims to be worth $700M cannot manage to pay an investor $3400 per month, that's the information we need.

I await your reply to all!
Respectfully
Pat Dougherty

No Response
Paul's weekly updates continue
Received from Paul on 10/20/23 (See original email on page 126)

> Dear Investors of ROI
>
> Please accept this letter as my continued effort to be transparent with you regarding the latest with ROI
>
> I understand that the former CEO of ROI has stated that ROI spent $1.8 million on the company. I have been away from the company for the last year but I do want all of you to know that JD Frost and his accounting team drafted a 2022 tax return that shows nearly 8X that was spent on ROI.
>
> In terms of ROI moving forward, I continue to be in discussions with potential investors to help ROI secure funding for new management. I am consumed with ROI and doing everything I can to keep this company moving forward.
>
> Sincerely
> Paul Croft

Narcissists play the Blame Game to protect their fragile egos and in this week's update he is clearly laying the blame for ROI's failure on the former CEO.

My reply to Paul and the Investors Group:

Paul,

Let me get this straight. In order to prove that everything is "fine" with ROI you are referencing tax returns prepared by a guy who is currently in default with my monthly interest payments, the guy who after going months without paying employees, shut the doors of his tax firm (your tax firm) without any notice to those employees or customers leaving everyone high and dry, the guy whose wife has filed for divorce, who's not returning calls and has gone silent (as you have) on all of his social media platforms, and the guy who's even been removed from the family business's website even though he's listed as the VP of the company, that's who you are referencing as your beacon of truth?

The guy who told me that he couldn't afford to pay my monthly stipend while standing on a golf course in Scotland, that guy? I'd give that an LOL if it wasn't so blatantly stupid!!!

To steal a line from the movie Jerry McGuire you need to "Show me the Money", Paul, because none of this dribble you're sending out in these late Friday emails is saying anything! If JD really did file taxes showing 8X more invested than the $1.8M, which totals $14.4M, and still leaves an estimated $36M unaccounted for, then we need to see it! And if ROI really is still on track, then we need to see the proof of that as well, because stating that

"In terms of ROI moving forward, I continue to be in discussion with potential investors to help ROI secure funding for new management" is just more tap dancing around the truth, we know it and you know it!

So, here's the thing, Paul, and I'm only speaking for myself here. I've got a file that's two inches thick and it contains hundreds of documents, emails, and text messages all bearing your name and signature and they clearly, CLEARLY, show deception. I'm going to give you one more week to "clarify" to me and the entire group of investors exactly what's going on and where our money is or where our money went, and if I don't get some answers, I'm going public with my information. And, trust me, it won't be the little Chattanooga Newspaper that I reach out to.

I look forward to honest information in next Friday's email.

Respectfully
Pat D

One week later:
Received from Paul on 10/27/23 (See original email on page 127)

Dear Investors of ROI

Please accept this letter as my continued effort to be transparent with you regarding the latest with ROI

I am pleased to report that I had a positive meeting with potential investors in ROI over the last week. I am reluctant to share more until the terms become memorialized. However, I will share that these potential investors see the vision, financial upside, and disruptive market force behind a hydrogen facility.

I know a lot of you are concerned about ROI based largely on what happened at the accounting firm of Croft & Frost. Please note that ROI is distinct from Croft & Frost. I continue to maintain a steadfast belief that ROI will flourish. The mission, technology, and strategy involved is at the forefront of a new chapter for our country and world.

Sincerely,
Paul Croft

I did not reply to this email because I felt it was just a regurgitation of an update he'd sent a couple weeks prior. He was running out of lies!

11/3/23: Another Friday and another update from Paul, this one claiming that he was in talks with potential investors and getting ROI back on track. At the same time, the Investors Group had already been made aware of at least two civil suits that had been filed claiming that Croft & Frost had defrauded people out of several hundred thousand dollars, so we knew that his claims of "discussions" with potential investors was a load of BS, because by this time there was no way anyone would give him a penny for an investment. But he was obviously trying to buy time, for what reason we really weren't sure.

I had now gone two months without a monthly interest payment so my financial stresses were mounting and my patience was running thin, but once again I decided not to reply.

Friday, November 17th, we received another update from Paul and for some reason this one really got under my skin! It was bad enough that the guy had defrauded almost 250 people, some out of their entire life savings, but to keep on trolling us with assertions that he was continuing to "work hard" trying to keep the company afloat was giving some in the Investors Group false hopes of regaining their investments and that pissed me off, so I replied to his email and really let him have it!

Received from Paul on 10/27/23 (See original email on page 128)

> Please accept this letter as my continued effort to be transparent with you regarding the latest with ROI
>
> I continue to work hard on keeping this company afloat and moving forward. Certain articles by the press lumping ROI with the issues that plagued the accounting company of Croft & Frost have slowed down the funding process. As I've explained to you all, ROI is a separate entity from Croft & Frost. Two separate entities with two

separate missions. I've explained this to potential investors to alleviate their concerns. In addition, to address their concerns that these funds will be used to bankroll anything other than ROI, I am more than open to placing the funds in a trust requiring oversight and approval before being released for legitimate ROI expenses. I am putting a lot of effort into ROI for all of us. I do feel bad that the company hit a rocky road while I was away on leave and desperately want to make the company thrive to benefit us as a whole.

I will not have an update next Friday due to the Thanksgiving holiday. My next update will be 12.1.23

Sincerely,
Paul Croft

My response sent to Paul the following day:

Once again, Paul, in the spirit of transparency, please advise on the following two new lawsuits filed this week:

Cook County IL Case No. 2023 L, VILHELM VENTURES SERIES E - Plaintiff vs JONA-THAN D. FROST - Defendant

Suit alleges that JD Frost has defaulted on a GUARANTEED return on a $500,000 investment in which defendant was supposedly going to sell 50 membership units in ROI

Cook County IL Case No 2023CH09344, ANGEL COLLOKU - Plaintiff vs CROFT & FROST, PLLC, PAUL CROFT, and JONATHAN FROST - Defendants

Class Action Suit alleges default on multiple investments into multiple businesses owned and operated by Paul Croft & JD Frost

Also, you and JD both sold some of your equity in ROI (see Cook County IL Case No. 2023 L above) which is why you guys face these subsequent lawsuits. The transparency that we investors want to know is where those funds went, because it's apparent that they did not go to fund ROI.

Your attached letter states that Croft & Frost Accounting and ROI are two separate entities with two separate missions, but from what I can tell they were both set up for one mission and that was to steal money from trusting investors while giving them nothing but empty promises in return. I think we all sincerely hope that other investors aren't being swindled like the rest of us were.

Fool me once, shame on you, fool me twice, shame on me, right?

You state that you'd be happy to oversee the trust to ensure that legitimate ROI expenses are paid and do not include a salary for you. It's been reported that while you were away "on leave" you were still collecting a healthy salary from ROI, sticking to your well documented motto about "paying yourself first." Have you liquidated all of your assets to begin paying back investors, like me, for the promissory notes that are beyond past due? If not then these weekly "updates" are nothing more than hollow words put together for what I can only assume is your attempt to buy time, something you are quickly running out of!

You purport to be a man of God so I will leave you with this. Proverbs 10:9 - Whoever walks in integrity walks securely, but whoever takes crooked paths will be found out. God is the way, the truth, and the light. Wrongdoing will always come to the light, which means cheating will always be discovered.

You, sir, have been discovered!

Sincerely
Pat D

Christianity was such a big component of his online persona that I thought I would call out the hypocrisy, probably didn't have much of an effect on him but it sure made me feel better!

As I said before, narcissists just don't know when to quit!!

Received from Paul on 12/1/23 (See original email on page 129)

> Please accept this letter as my continued effort to be transparent with you regarding the latest with ROI
>
> Unfortunately, I do not have the news I wanted to share in this letter post-Thanksgiving. I remain in active discussions with potential investors. In fact, I am currently in the Northeast engaging in these discussions in person, day and night. I am working hard on securing additional investment funds in ROI to keep the company moving forward. I hope to have some good news on this front shortly.
>
> Sincerely,
> Paul Croft

My reply on 12/2/23:

> Once again, Paul, I cannot thank you enough for your continued due diligence in working to fund for ROI, knowing that you are out there "day and night", like Batman & Robin, makes me sleep a whole lot better! Instead of a Bat Signal maybe we can get a spotlight in Gotham City to send out a "Paul Signal" notifying you of where investors are lining up in the North East, could be a real time saver!

As we prepare to celebrate the birth of Jesus Christ, I thought it might be a good time to see just how well you're doing with the 10 commandments:

- You shall have no other Gods before me: It's quite apparent that the almighty dollar is your one and only true god so this is a **FAIL**

- Thou shalt not make unto thee any graven images: You cherish Mansions, Boats, Ferraris over the cross so this is a **FAIL**

- Thou shalt not take the name of the Lord thy God in vain: You hold the bible high while cheating people out of their life savings so this is a **FAIL**

- Remember the Sabbath day and keep it Holy: If I had any money left I'd bet that you've lied and cheated on Sundays so this is another **FAIL**

- Honor your father and mother: From what I've heard and read your folks are absolutely ashamed of you so this is a **FAIL**

- Thou shalt not kill: We'll assume **PASS** on this one but finding out otherwise wouldn't surprise me one bit

- Thou shalt not commit adultery: Adultery doesn't have to be of the flesh, smacking your wife around also qualifies so it's another **FAIL**

- Thou shalt not steal: **LOL!!! FAIL**

- Thou shall not bear false witness: See Commandments 1-8 **FAIL**

- Thou shall not covet: I spent 50 years saving for retirement and you stole it so **FAIL FAIL FAIL**

Proverbs 21:6 - A fortune made by a lying tongue is a fleeting vapor and a deadly snare

I think you'll like prison, Paul. You get three hot meals a day, the open-air steel toilets leave no secrets between you and your "bunk buddy", and I think there's even a chance that you'll end up rooming with the guy who has the most cigarettes, so that's definitely something to look forward to! They even have your prison yearbook photo ready to go! SEE BELOW!

Merry Christmas Paul!
Pat D

The next day I received a threatening text from an Officer Hickland who claimed to be from the Department of Homeland Security. His text stated that he was contacting me regarding the defamation of Paul Croft in email chains and social media and that they were preparing to press charges against me if my email replies to Paul didn't stop. The text also contained 3-4 bullet points that outlined the defamation of character. (See original texts on pages 130-131)

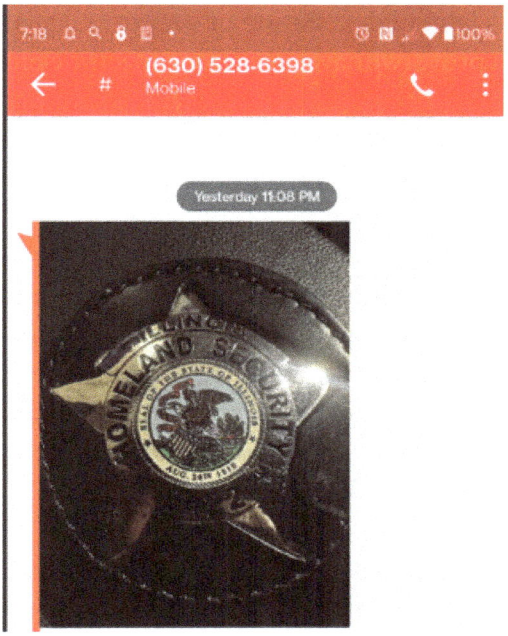

Good evening, Patrick Dougherty, my name is Officer Hickland. I'm asking that you do not contact Paul Croft or include any threats or allegations through any chain of email or social media. You have broken all claims of defamation of character and we're prepared to press charges against you if this continues. Thank you and have a great night.

The Text Continues:

Elements of Defamation of Character. To prevail on a claim of defamation of character, a plaintiff must prove (we have proof) four specific elements:

1) You made a false statement about the plaintiff. The plaintiff has the burden of proving that the statement was false.

2) The statement was made publicly, meaning it could not be made in a private conversation between you and the plaintiff. In addition to establishing that others heard or read the statement, the plaintiff must prove that it could be reasonably interpreted as disparaging.

3) You acted with malice, or negligence as to the falsity of the statement. The plaintiff must prove that you knew, or should have known, that the statement was false and was likely to cause harm to the plaintiff

4) The plaintiff suffered actual damages as a result of the statement. This means damages can be expressed in monetary terms and are directly attributable to the statement.

I have to admit that this text caught me completely off guard but to me this was nothing more than just another attempt by Paul to bully and manipulate me and I wasn't having any of it! So, I immediately replied back in an email, once again copying the entire Investors Group, and included screenshots of the DHS

Badge along with the text message. I can't tell you how happy it made me to know that I was getting under Paul's very thin skin! Here's my response:

> Once again, Paul, thank you for your continued efforts in acquiring funding for the ROI project and the "transparency" in keeping us informed. Your most recent letter states that you remain open to answering questions to the best of your knowledge so please update us on the multiple lawsuits filed against you and JD and where the two of you are at in those legal processes, I'm sure we would all appreciate it.
>
> I also wanted to let you know that I was able to find the exact same Homeland Security Badge you sent in your recent threatening text at my local Party City, so next Halloween everyone can dress up like Officer Hickland, how much fun will that be?
>
> I wish you and JD a very blessed Christmas and hope that you get everything that you deserve, not only from Santa, but also from the DOJ, you both deserve it!
>
> Pat D

Obviously, these emails had gotten a bit out of control and it was at this time that I was contacted privately by one of the investors and asked to stop the weekly back and forth with Paul. Even though the chances of recovering any of our investments were slim to none, it was this investor's opinion that my tart email responses were not doing anything to help our situation so, respecting his wishes, I agreed to end my email "battle" with Paul.

Over the six weeks of email exchanges, I had received dozens of private messages from frustrated investors, thanking me for responding to Paul, and for not letting him indiscriminately troll us with his weekly bullshit updates. Included on the copy list were a couple of law firms involved in various suits against Croft & Frost, and a few of their people also contacted me with their approval, saying that the emails had been circulated throughout their organizations to everyone's delight, so that was kind of cool!

Looking back, I think that some of me replies may have been a bit childish, but at the same time I think I got my point across, and in the end that's all that mattered to me! They didn't cost me anything but time, and now that I'm broke and unretired, time seems to be in abundance so I may as well use it up!

Homeland Security

After learning about the fake homeland security text one of the Law Firms in Chicago filed a report with the Illinois State Police. I was then contacted by someone at the law firm and given the name and number of an Illinois State Trooper who, I was told, would be contacting me within a few days. About 5-6 weeks went by and I hadn't heard anything from the trouper so I decided to give him a call.

He answered the phone right away, and once I had identified myself and explained who I was and why I was calling, he acknowledged the situation and told me that he had contacted Walter Hickland, who apparently is a friend of Paul's from Plainfield, IL, and that he had admitted to sending the threatening text as a favor to Paul. The trouper told me that after a long talk with Mr. Hickland he said he wouldn't do it again. And, apparently, that was that!

This was not the answer I was looking for and I let the trouper know how disappointed I was in his lack of action! I reminded him of the threatening nature of the text, that Mr. Hickland was aiding someone who was under investigation for fraud in multiple states, and that impersonating a police officer is a federal crime, punishable up to three years in prison and a fine, and I didn't think that having a "little talk" with Walter Hickland was sufficient action for what was clearly an egregious violation of the law.

I also asked if he had spoken to Paul Croft and he responded that he hadn't which, again, did not sit well with me!

After a 20-minute discussion the trooper promised that he would do more follow up but as of today, six months later, I haven't heard anything back on the subject, so I'm thinking that the Illinois State Police have closed this one out. Paul has been doing business in the Chicago area for a couple of decades and I'm sure that, over time, he has made many connections in high places of power. I would like to think that the State Police did not brush any of this under the rug as a favor to Paul but at this point nothing would surprise me. Pretty sad!

The Wheels of Justice

It's now been one year since Croft & Frost closed its doors and civilly there's been a lot that's happened. Paul and JD, individually and combined, are facing multiple lawsuits, including a Class Action Suit brought by our Investor's Group, claiming fraud on various investment schemes and, after admitting to those schemes, the State of Tennessee has revoked JD's CPA License.

According to an article from Pressreader.com/Chattanooga-times-free-press, dated February 27th, 2024, the Tennessee State Board of Accountancy stated that Frost had violated at least eight state rules or statutes including bans on "Dishonesty, fraud, or gross negligence in performance of services." In signing the consent form, Frost admitted to the allegations, and in doing so, avoided civil penalties by the regulatory agency over the specific complaints.

Andrew Schwartz and Sofia Saric are great reporters at The Chattanooga Times Free Press and they have been all over this story from day one. You can get more information on the ongoing Croft & Frost story at https://www.timesfreepress.com.

Paul resides in Chicago which is a much larger pond than Chattanooga, so there seems to be little news of anything happening with him. As I pointed out before, he is listed with JD as the co-defendant in multiple lawsuits, but searching for articles on Paul yield little news outside of what's already been reported by the Times Free Press. CBS Channel 2 in Chicago did a recent report on the ROI fraud so hopefully the authorities are finally taking steps against Paul Croft as well.

Here is the link to that report.

> https://www.youtube.com/
> watch?v=WZ2fXQkpep0

Forbes has also done some investigative reporting on the ROI Scheme and I am including links to their written and video reports below.

> https://mail.google.com/mail/u/0/#inbox/FMf
> cgzGxStpPHBhplPVqscLlGVPDBfsx?projector
> =1&messagePartId=0.1

> https://www.youtube.com/
> watch?v=ej1k4GZLiWU

I'll be honest, as a victim I want revenge on Paul and JD, but I also want them to be held accountable for the crimes they've committed. Before investing in ROI, I told JD all about my life and how hard I had worked to put away my little nest egg. He knew I was counting on that money in my retirement and yet, after assuring me that investing with him and Paul was safe, he turned around and started spending my savings on his personal vacations and golf outings! I think he had no intentions of investing my money in any type of renewable energy business at all, his only goal was to con me out of my retirement funds so that he could "appear" to live the high life!

And they both held the bible high while cheating people which I find to be reprehensible but, knowing what I know now, I'm not surprised!

Famed Ponzi Schemer Bernie Madoff was found guilty of defrauding investors out of an estimated $20B and he was sentenced to 150 years in prison, I see no difference in what he did to his investors and what Paul and JD did to us. They knowingly lied to investors and used our money to fund their lavish lifestyles and they need to be held criminally accountable for their actions. After a few Skype meetings and several group emails I think the Investors Group understands that our money is gone and there's very little chance we'll get any of it back. But if you took a poll of the group, I'm confident that the majority of us would like to see Paul and JD meet the same fate as Madoff, Tom Petters, or the guy that got it all started, Charles Ponzi himself.

Personally, I will continue to follow these two as the story unfolds and hopefully the day will come when they face judgement in criminal court, and when that day comes, I plan on being there to extract a little bit of satisfaction, it's about the only thing I have a real chance of walking away with out of this tangled mess!

Summary

Putting my story out for all to read was a tough decision for me. Outside of confiding in a few close friends I haven't told anyone that I got caught up in all of this. I've always taken pride in my ability to read people and the fact that I allowed someone like JD Frost to con me is embarrassing. How could I have been so gullible, so naive, so stupid? I saw dollar signs and was done in by greed, plain and simple.

I also haven't told my family, especially my kids, because I don't want anyone worrying about me, I'm the one that fucked up so I should be the one who has to deal with all the sleepless nights!

Thankfully, I didn't allow them to talk me out of my pension, because if they had this story would have a completely different ending. I'm guaranteed a monthly pension payment that, when combined with my social security and some part time income, is enough to live comfortably on. I also have other investments so they didn't get it all, thank God.

But my retirement is gone, it bought Paul Croft a sports car and paid for JD Frost's dream golf trip to Scotland, glad I could help them out.

50 years of working my ass off and I got a grand total of nine months of retirement, doesn't seem fair but it's what I get for being an idiot!

But I'll be okay. I've spent my entire life as a middle-class worker bee and always intended on working part time in retirement, so I'll continue to get up at 5:00 AM, go to work, and things will be fine. Before retiring in 2022 I made sure to clean up some debt so I'm sitting pretty good in that regard, the only unknown is how things shake out with the new cabin. I will do whatever I can to keep it but if it gets to be too much of a burden then I may have to let that go, but that's a decision I'll address if and when the time comes.

But I'm afraid I'll have to say goodbye to some of those dreams I shared with you earlier in this text. Ireland, the Swiss Alps, Italy, Alaska, and Hawaii are all more than likely out of reach for me now. So is that Candy Apple Red, 1969, Nova SS which is a shame because I would have looked damn good in that thing!

But there's still lots of places to go and see right here in the U.S., so now I'm looking forward to road trips to Yellowstone and Glacier, Yosemite, MOAB in Utah, and I really want to see the Blue Ridge Mountains and stay in Asheville NC, the pictures I've seen from that area of the country look amazing.

And instead of listening to Traditional Irish Music while sipping a Guiness in a Pub in Ireland, I might have to settle for having a Bourbon on the rocks while listening to some good old Country Music at a Honky-Tonk in Nashville. That wouldn't be so bad.

My kids and grandkids are doing great so I'm very happy about that! I'm in good health, both physically and mentally, and I'm blessed with great family and friends who give me love and support every day, so I may not be financially wealthy but in many ways I'm still a rich man.

These past couple of years have been a real struggle for me. Like a juggler keeping multiple balls in the air, I was dealing with all the Paul and JD bullshit on one side while keeping up my normal happy go lucky, everything is great, front for my family and friends, not giving them any inkling of what was going on with my life.

Internally I was struggling, too, with feelings that weren't consistent with my personality. Those that know me best would probably describe me as loving, caring, and sympathetic, but the emotions that I've constantly dealt with these past two years were anger and rage. I hated the two of them for what they did to me and I wanted revenge, still do.

Eventually, I realized that all my hate wasn't hurting Paul and JD, not in the least bit, but it was definitely taking its toll on me, and after letting those two assholes steal my money, I couldn't afford to let them take my soul too, it just wasn't worth it!

So, I decided to let it go, I had too.

Fifty years of hard work, minding my Ps & Qs and keeping my nose to the grind stone, only to be defrauded out of everything by a couple of Wolves in Sheep's Clothing, definitely wasn't part of my master plan. But at the end of the day at least I can look at myself in the mirror and still see an honest and decent man who's loved and respected, and that's a hell of a lot more than can be said about Paul Thomas Croft and Jonathan David Frost!

Thanks for taking the time to read my story and have a Great Day!

Pat D

Thanks

I would like to thank my kids, Abby & Justin and Patrick & Ellie, for all the love they give me each and every day, becoming a dad was the best thing that ever happened to me.

Thanks to my Grandkids Riley, Gannon, Eloise, Evelyn, and Tatum for all the great hugs and kisses, you fill my heart with joy!

Thanks to my family and friends for their lifetime of support, you all mean the world to me! And a special thanks to Maggie for her honest assessment of my writing skills, I can't tell you how much I valued your opinion.

And, finally, to everyone who supported me through the years, those I worked with or for, if it wasn't for great people like you I would never have made it through 50+ years, so thank you!

Evidence

From: ~~Jorindacasanova@crof~~
Sent: Tuesday, November 2, 2021 10:03 PM
To: Patrick Dougherty ~~~~
Subject: [EXTERNAL] Investment Options

Hi there –

The attached is approved by Paul. This gives you several options should you want to retire now from 3M. In my opinion, Options 2, 3, or 4 are the best. I listed all to be sure we did our due diligence. Let me know what you think. We can also structure Option #4 with more or less per month. This will just affect the Lump Sum Payment. Thank you!

~~~~

Building Courage. Creating Wealth.

~~~~

Business Development Administrator

d. 651-724-1413 | o. 423-486-9200

375 Jackson Street, Suite 700 E, St. Paul, MN 55101

www.croftandfrost.com

1

91

Patrick Dougherty
One Year Return of 100%; Subsequent Years - Simple Interest @ 12% for 3-5 Years

Option #1 - Five-Year Investment

Investment Amount $350,000	Initial Investment		% Return
November 2022 - Year 1 Return: 100%	$	350,000	100%
November 2023 - Year 2 Return: 12% Simple Interest	$	700,000	12%
November 2024 - Year 3 Return: 12% Simple Interest	$	700,000	12%
November 2025 - Year 4 Return: 12% Simple Interest	$	700,000	12%
November 2026 - Year 5 Return: 12% Simple Interest	$	700,000	12%

Option #2 - One-Year Investment

Investment Amount $350,000	Initial Investment		% Return
November 2022 - Year 1 Return: 100%	$	350,000	100%

Option #3 - Three-Year Investment - Take Disbursement of Original Investment Amount of $350,000

Investment Amount $350,000	Initial Investment		% Return
November 2022 - Year 1 Return: 100%	$	350,000	100%
November 2023 - Year 2 Return: 12% Simple Interest on Year-One % Return Amount of $350,000	$	350,000	12%
November 2024 - Year 3 Return: 12% Simple Interest on Year-One % Return Amount of $350,000	$	350,000	12%

Option #4 - Five-Year Investment w/Monthly Payments beginning November 2022

Investment Amount $350,000	Initial Investment		% Return
November 2022 - Year 1 Return: 100%	$	350,000	100%
November 2023 - Year 2 Return: 12% - Disbursement of Return for 12 Months	$	700,000	12%
November 2024 - Year 3 Return: 12% - Disbursement of Return for 12 Months	$	700,000	12%
November 2025 - Year 2 Return: 12% - Disbursement of Return for 12 Months	$	700,000	12%
November 2026 - Year 2 Return: 12% - Disbursement of Return for 12 Months	$	700,000	12%

Return Amount		Total	
$	350,000	$	700,000
$	84,000	$	784,000
$	84,000	$	868,000
$	84,000	$	952,000
$	84,000	$	1,036,000 Total Lump Sum Payment

Return Amount		Total	
$	350,000	$	700,000 Total Lump Sum Payment

Return Amount		Total	
$	350,000	$	700,000 Disbursement of $350,000 Original Investment Amount
$	42,000	$	392,000
$	42,000	$	434,000 Total Lump Sum Payment

Return Amount		Monthly Withdrawal Amount of Yearly Return Amount Divided by 12 Months		Total	
$	350,000			$	700,000
$	84,000	$	7,000	$	700,000
$	84,000	$	7,000	$	700,000
$	84,000	$	7,000	$	700,000
$	84,000	$	7,000	$	700,000 Total Lump Sum Payment

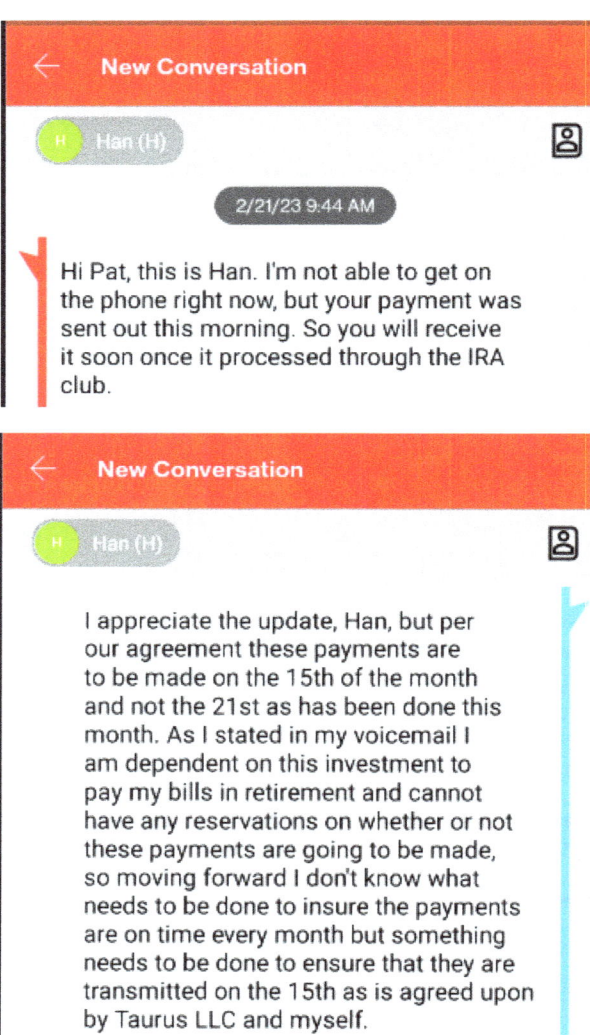

New Conversation

Han (H)

2/21/23 9:44 AM

Hi Pat, this is Han. I'm not able to get on the phone right now, but your payment was sent out this morning. So you will receive it soon once it processed through the IRA club.

New Conversation

Han (H)

I appreciate the update, Han, but per our agreement these payments are to be made on the 15th of the month and not the 21st as has been done this month. As I stated in my voicemail I am dependent on this investment to pay my bills in retirement and cannot have any reservations on whether or not these payments are going to be made, so moving forward I don't know what needs to be done to insure the payments are on time every month but something needs to be done to ensure that they are transmitted on the 15th as is agreed upon by Taurus LLC and myself.

We have 41 months to go and the fact that we've had so many issues in the first 6 months does not give me a sense of security on this!

2/21/23 9:59 AM

I understand your concerns and this is temporary as we are working on getting our ROI project fully funded. These delays will be resolved very soon going forward.

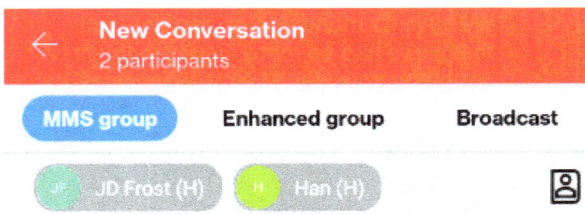

New Conversation
2 participants

MMS group   **Enhanced group**   **Broadcast**

JD Frost (H)   Han (H)

4/20/23 8:53 AM

Good morning, Han, hope you are well. Pat Dougherty here with a friendly reminder that it's the 20th of the month so please make sure my monthly payment is made to the IRA Club today, thanks!

4/20/23 10:33 AM

JD Frost

Hey Pat we should have that ready at the latest next Friday

Next Friday is the 27th and my deposit from the IRA Club is made on the 28th so that's not going to work, can it be made by next Monday the 24th?

Delivered

JD Frost

We will do our best

JD Frost (H)

We are sending to IRA Club today this morning

5/1/23 10:09 AM

As we discussed last Friday the promissory note states a grace of 10 days and after that the borrower pays the lender a 2% late fee so that's an extra $68.00, will that be included?

5/1/23 10:21 AM

We are sending the payment to IrA club today

Yes

5/1/23 4:42 PM

Your payment was released today with the penalty amount

Should be there today or tomorrow

Thank you for your patience

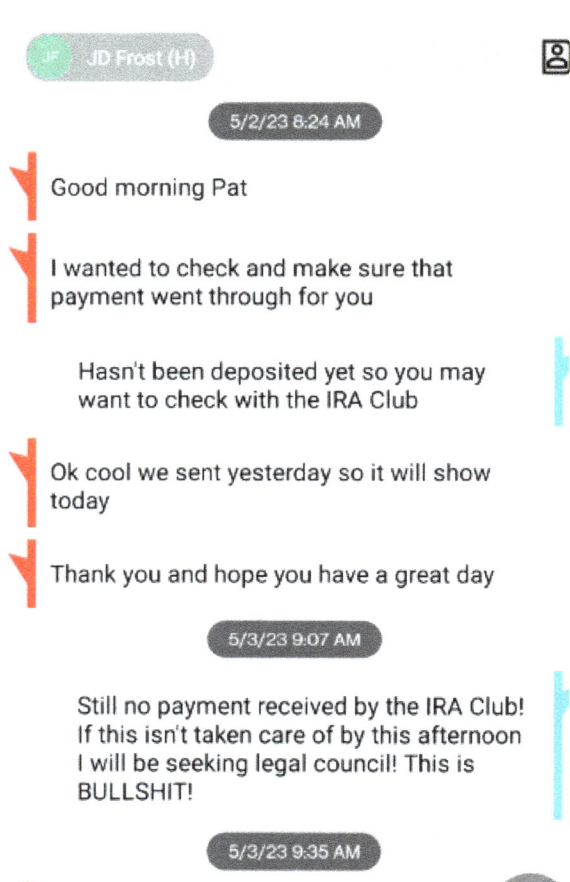

JD Frost (H)

5/2/23 8:24 AM

Good morning Pat

I wanted to check and make sure that payment went through for you

Hasn't been deposited yet so you may want to check with the IRA Club

Ok cool we sent yesterday so it will show today

Thank you and hope you have a great day

5/3/23 9:07 AM

Still no payment received by the IRA Club! If this isn't taken care of by this afternoon I will be seeking legal council! This is BULLSHIT!

5/3/23 9:35 AM

I believe we have the issue figured out

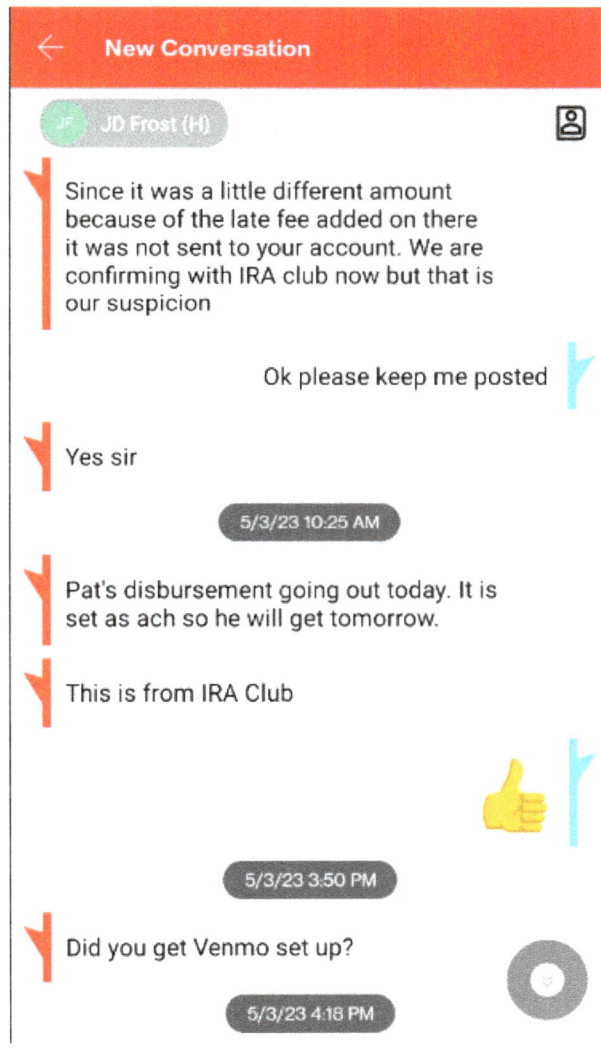

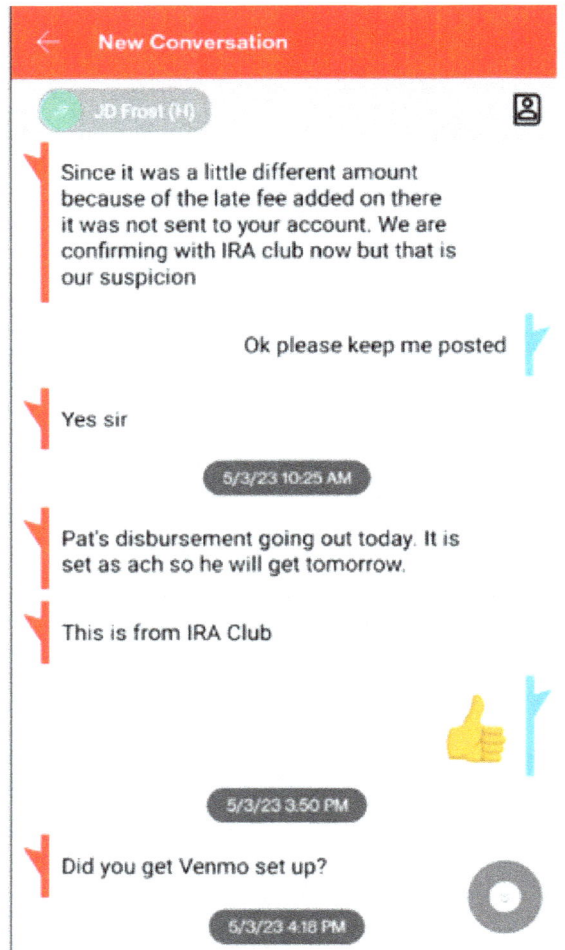

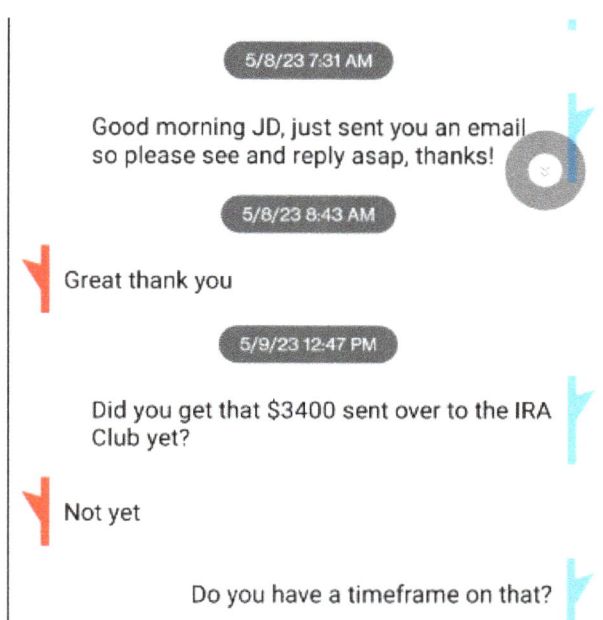

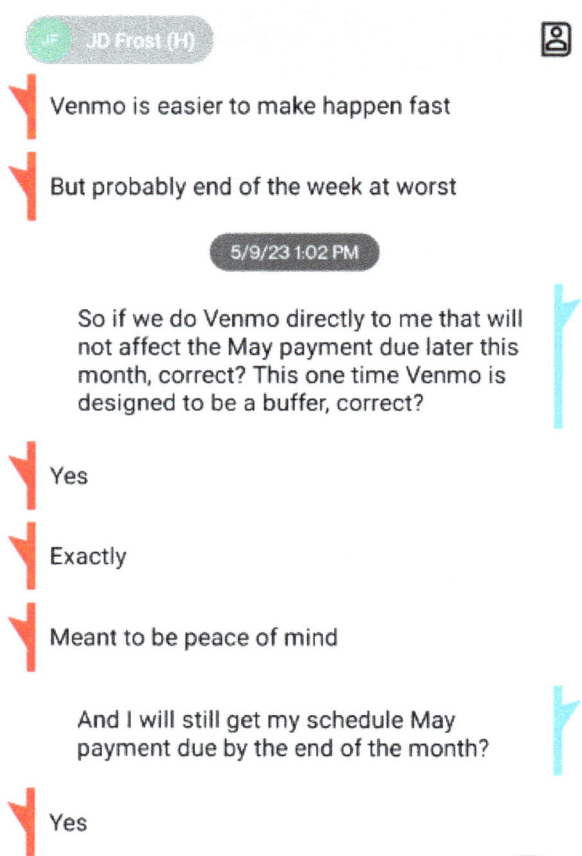

JD Frost (H)

Venmo is easier to make happen fast

But probably end of the week at worst

5/9/23 1:02 PM

So if we do Venmo directly to me that will not affect the May payment due later this month, correct? This one time Venmo is designed to be a buffer, correct?

Yes

Exactly

Meant to be peace of mind

And I will still get my schedule May payment due by the end of the month?

Yes

Ok, so what do you need to know about my Venmo account to send me the money?

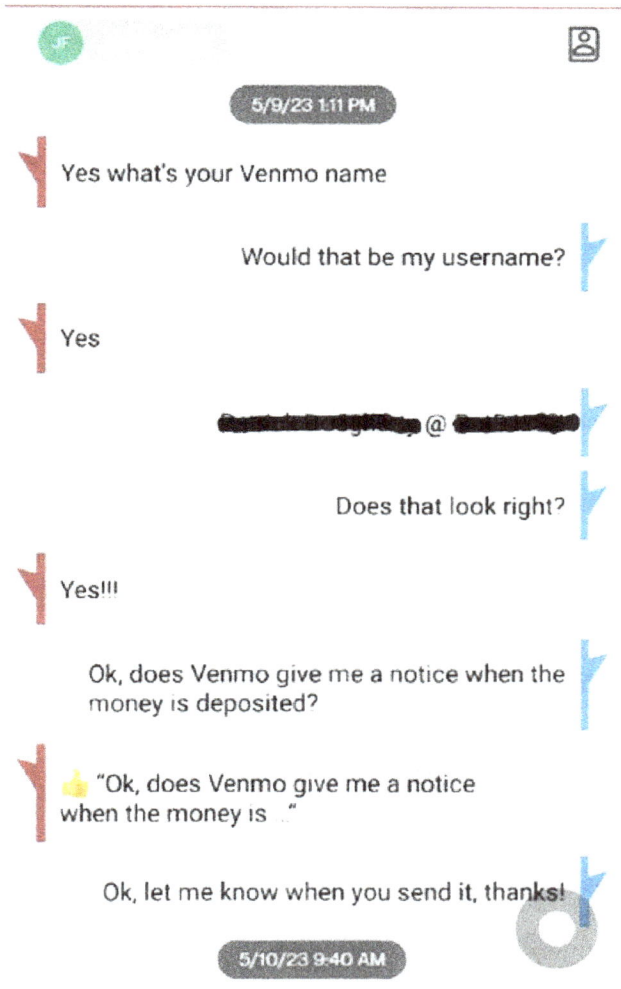

 JD Frost (H)

5/10/23 9:40 AM

That $505.00 was received by Venmo and successfully deposited to my bank account so go ahead and send the remaining $2895.00, thanks! 🙂

Will do if it lets me send

5/11/23 8:38 AM

On a different note are we going to send the remaining $2895.00 to my Venmo?

Just tried sending another $1,000 and it did not go through. Sometimes Venmo limits you on the amount you can send on a weekly basis. We will get it done

Just sent another $1,000

I was reading all the rules and regs on the Venmo sight and it states that individual payments up to $5000.00 can be made so something doesn't add up on that. Please keep trying and let me know when it goes through

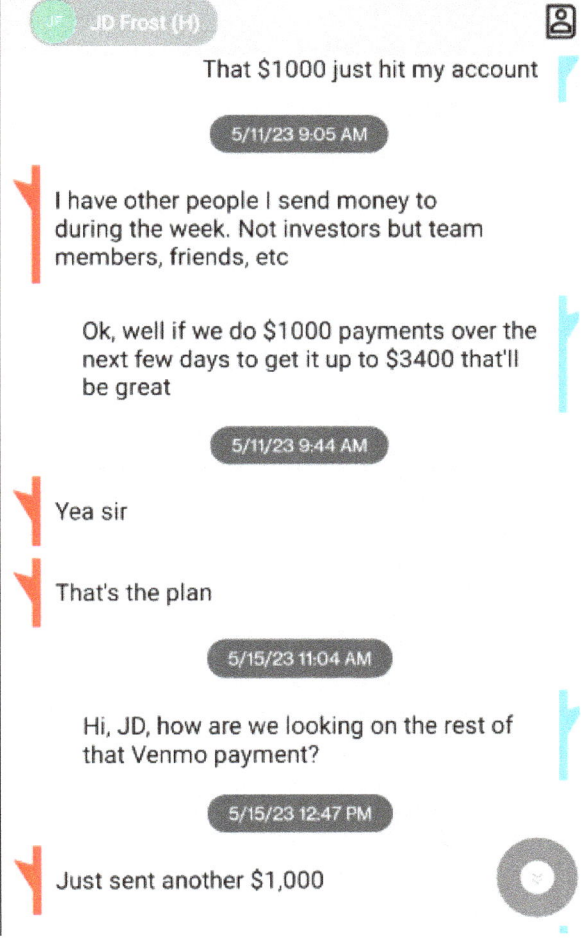

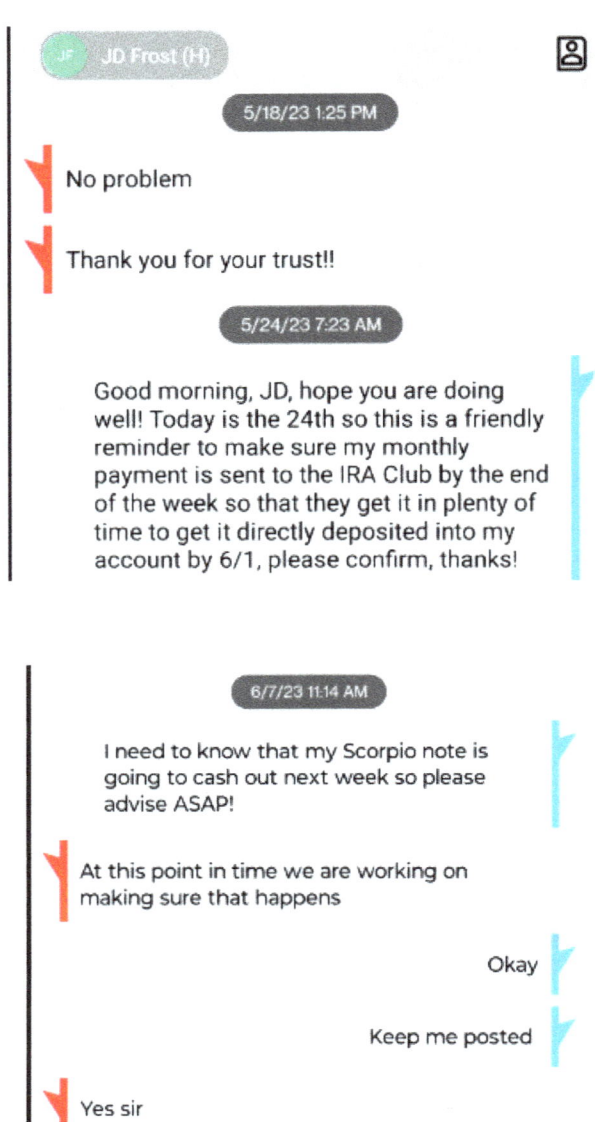

JF JD Frost (H)

5/18/23 1:25 PM

No problem

Thank you for your trust!!

5/24/23 7:23 AM

Good morning, JD, hope you are doing well! Today is the 24th so this is a friendly reminder to make sure my monthly payment is sent to the IRA Club by the end of the week so that they get it in plenty of time to get it directly deposited into my account by 6/1, please confirm, thanks!

6/7/23 11:14 AM

I need to know that my Scorpio note is going to cash out next week so please advise ASAP!

At this point in time we are working on making sure that happens

Okay

Keep me posted

Yes sir

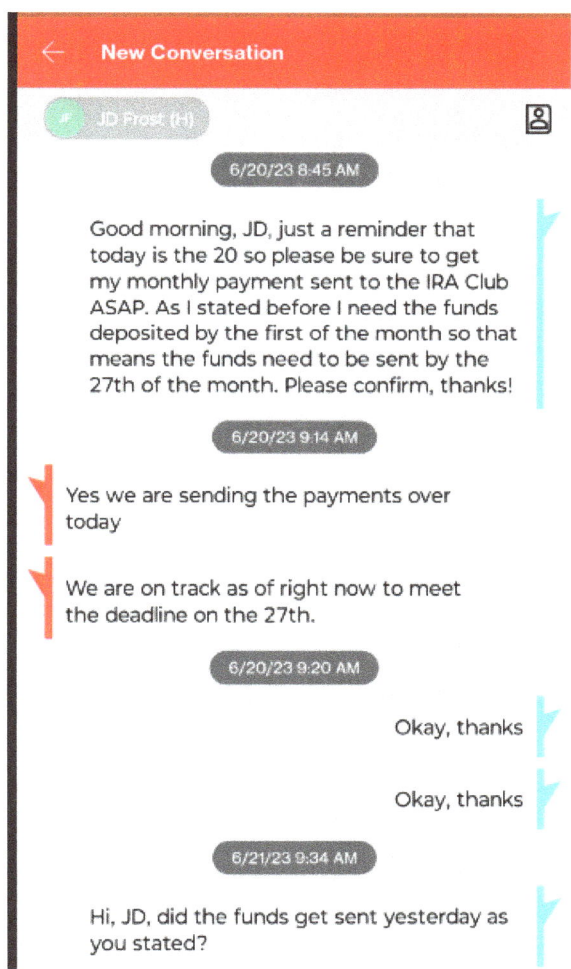

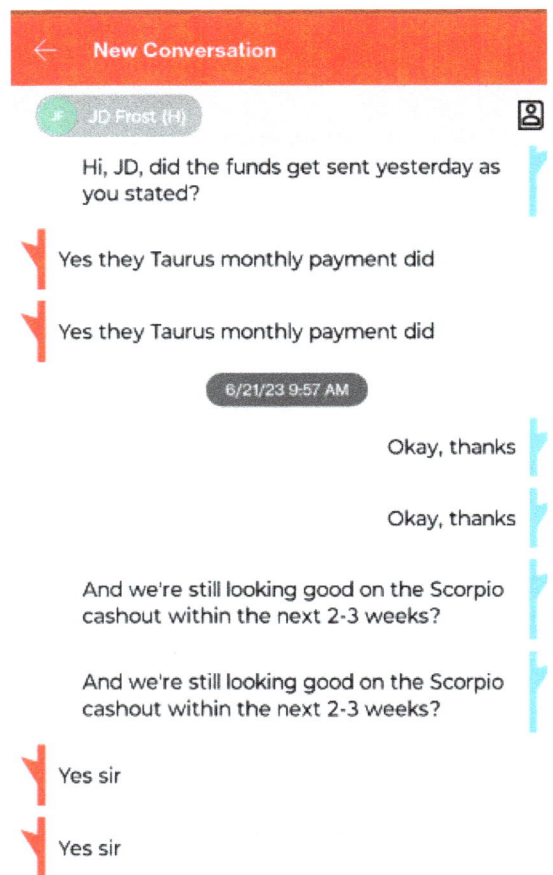

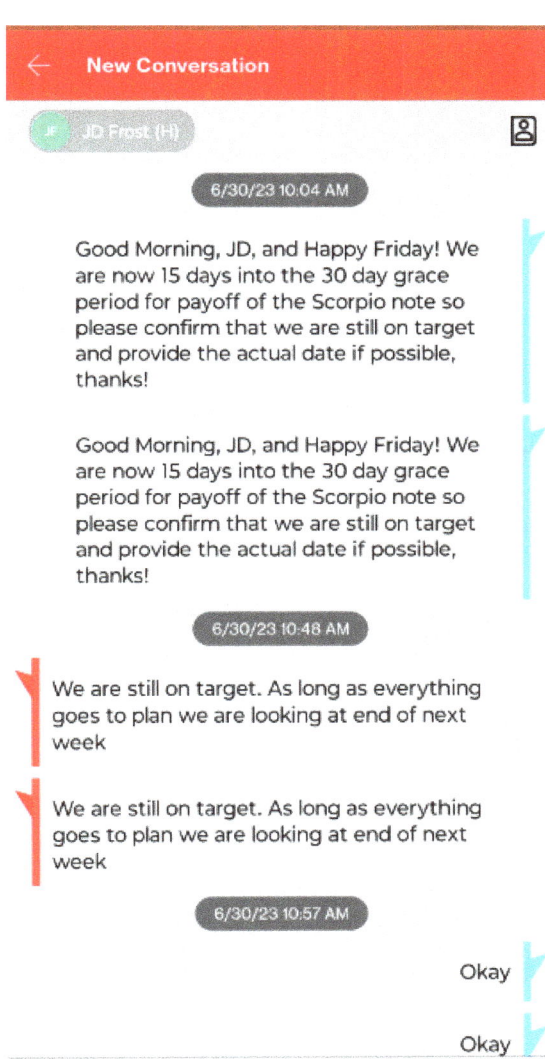

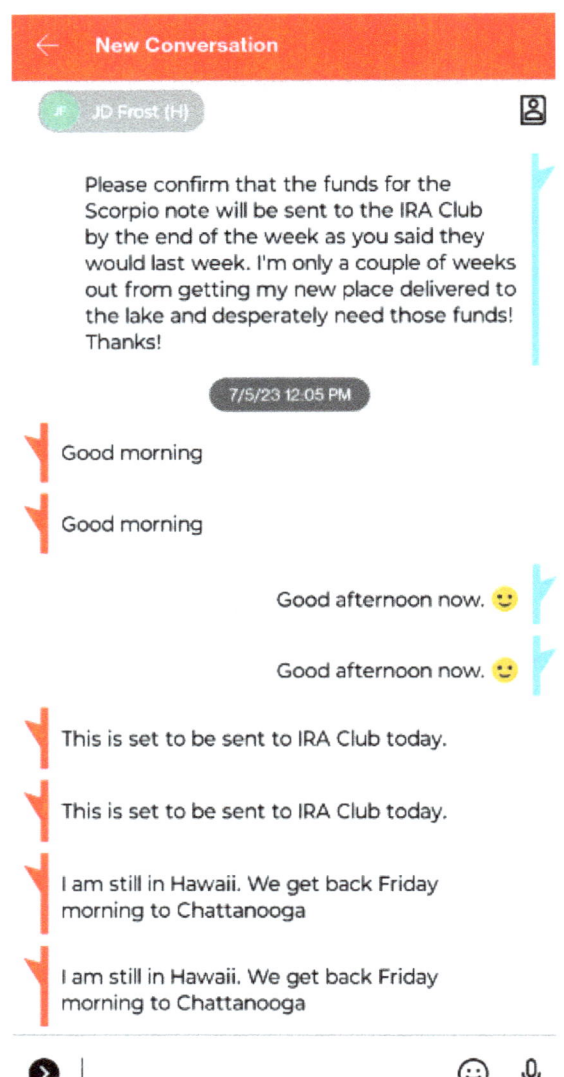

$50,400.00 going to my IRA Club Account today?

$50,400.00 going to my IRA Club Account today?

Yes sir

Yes sir

Great! I will follow up with Lisa then and thank you for your attention to this. I wish you and your family safe travels back to TN!

Great! I will follow up with Lisa then and thank you for your attention to this. I wish you and your family safe travels back to TN!

Thank you buddy

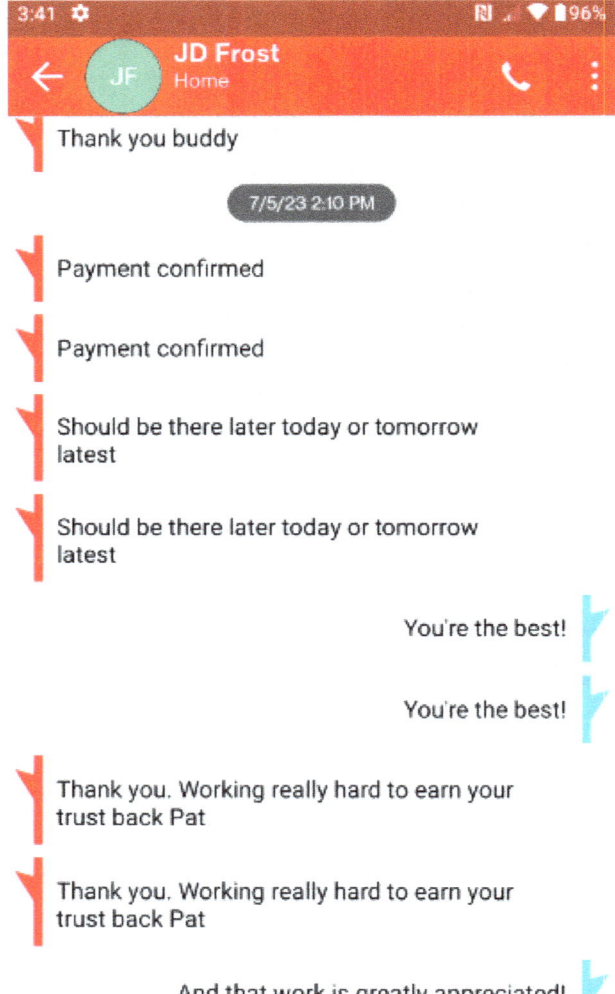

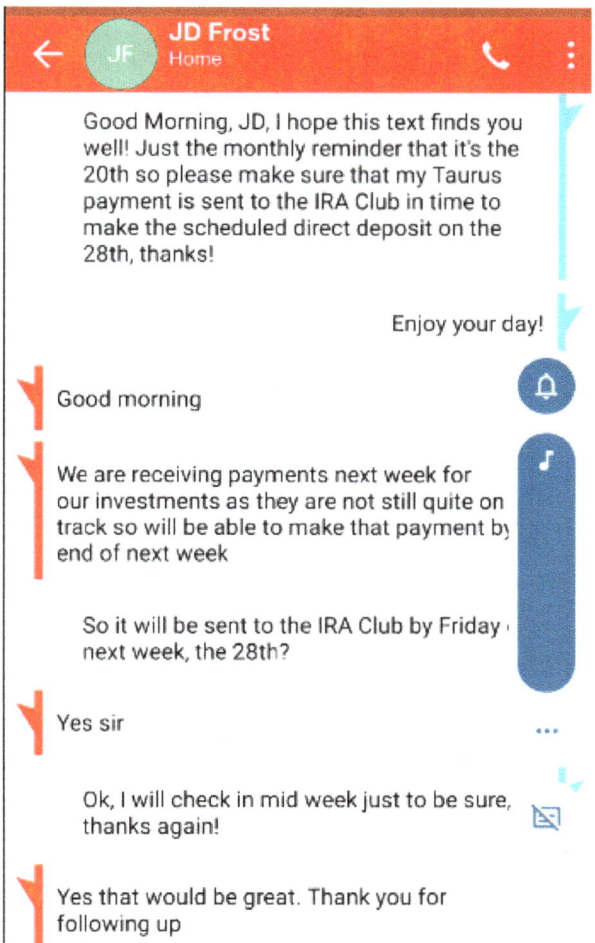

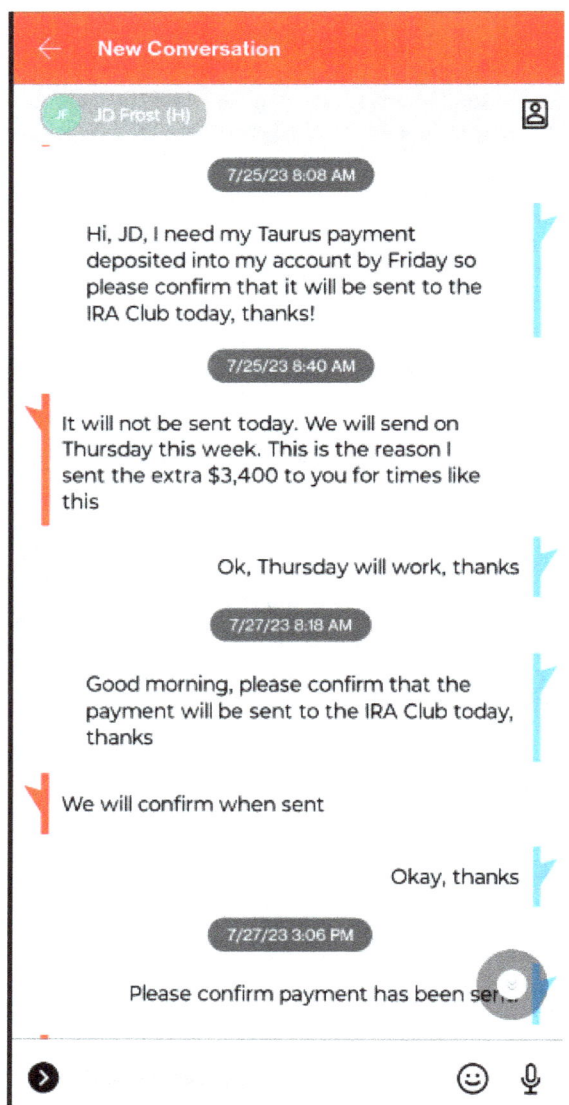

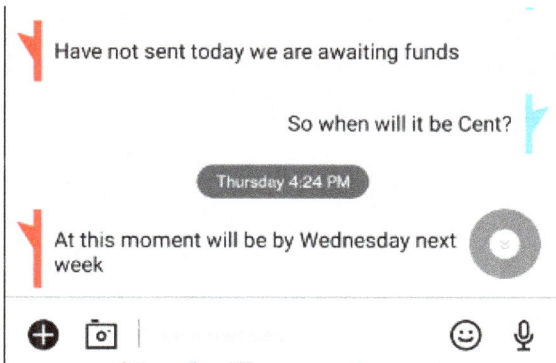

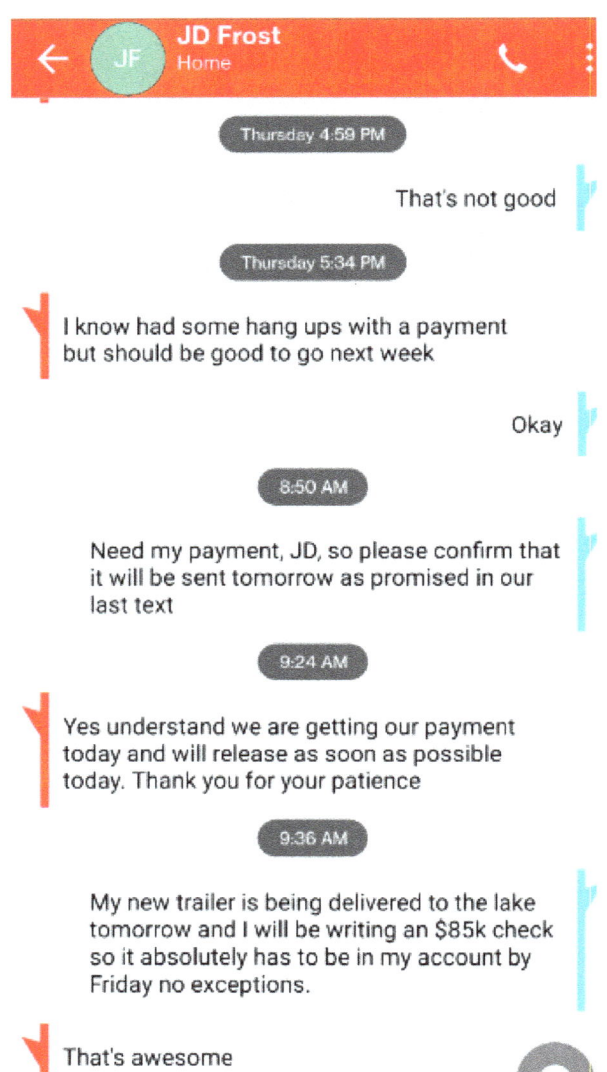

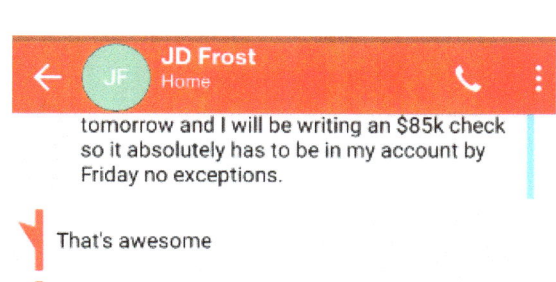

JD Frost
Home

tomorrow and I will be writing an $85k check so it absolutely has to be in my account by Friday no exceptions.

That's awesome

Pat I am not creating exceptions.

9:49 AM

I am about to take on an additional debt of roughly $70K and am looking at a monthly payment of close to $1K a month which was not budgeted for when I tried so now, in order to keep my cabin at the lake, I have to rely on my investment with you consistently paying out by the first of every month, otherwise my place at the lake will be gone.

You have a lake home so you understand the value they bring to our family and friends

👍 "I am about to take on an additional debt of roughl..."

Yes of course

JD Frost (H)

And we will make it happen for you

Thanks

8/2/23 8:04 AM

Good morning, just checking in on my
payment, will it be sent to the IRA Club today?

Yes

8/3/23 8:51 AM

No payment was sent to the IRA Club
yesterday, are you going to meet your
obligations or not?

We had to send it today. It's a long story

Yes we are going to meet our obligations

Do you still have the extra $3,400 I sent you
personally?

JD Frost (H)

Yes but when you sent that we agreed it would not change the structure of the monthly payments. It's not that I can't meet my obligations because I do pull off that 3400 and then replenish when I get my actual payment but the continued struggle with getting this done on time is extremely frustrating and we have to find a solution

I'm off to the lake so I'll be offline, please make sure that goes today

8/3/23 9:05 AM

Doing everything we can to ensure it goes today

8/3/23 4:54 PM

Did it get sent?

Yes sir

JD Frost
Home

9/14/23 3:23 PM

So is my investment secure or am I shit out of luck?

9/14/23 3:41 PM

I am seeking council this week. We will have better answers soon

Ok, well please keep me posted because I believed in you and I sure hope you don't let me down

I know you do and I appreciate that

Monday 9:16 AM

Good morning JD, hope you were able to enjoy some of your weekend. It's the 18th and I need to know if you're going to be able to make the monthly payment by the first of October and please be honest with me, thanks.

6:08 PM

Just drove two hours to get to my cabin, I need to know if you are going to meet your obligation and get me my monthly payment or if you're not. The only way I can keep this place is if I get my interest payments on a regular monthly basis.

Sent

120

Pat Dougherty <███████████████>   Tue, Aug 29, 2023 at 10:00 AM
To: Jonathan Frost <jdfrost@croftandfrost.com>
Cc: Matt Dira <██████@███████████>

Good Morning JD,

Please provide me with an updated account report showing gains from Q2.

Thanks!

Pat D

Jonathan Frost <jfrost@frostcpas.com>   Tue, Aug 29, 2023 at 10:07 AM
To: Pat Dougherty <███████████████████>
Cc: Jonathan Frost <jdfrost@croftandfrost.com>, Matt Dira <██████@████████████>

We will. Matt will put this together

Jonathan Frost

> On Aug 29, 2023, at 11:01 AM, Pat Dougherty <████████████@████████████> wrote:
>
>
>
[Quoted text hidden]

Pat Dougherty <███████████████████>   Tue, Aug 29, 2023 at 10:20 AM
To: Jonathan Frost <jfrost@frostcpas.com>
Cc: Jonathan Frost <jdfrost@croftandfrost.com>, Matt Dira <██████@████████████>

Ok, thanks.
[Quoted text hidden]

Matt Dira <████████████████████>   Tue, Aug 29, 2023 at 2:08 PM
To: Pat Dougherty <█████████████@████████>, Jonathan Frost <jfrost@frostcpas.com>
Cc: Jonathan Frost <jdfrost@croftandfrost.com>

Hey Pat,

Please see attached Q2 Account Statement.

Let me know if you have any questions.

Thanks,
Matt

STATEMENT OF ACCOUNT
Pat Dougherty

DATE	DESCRIPTION	CREDIT	DEBIT	ACCOUNT BALANCE
8/9/21	Promissory Note 1 (Note 1) W/ ($580,000) paid on 8/09/26	$250,000.00		$250,000.00
8/15/21	Note 1 Interest earned	$20,833.33		$270,833.33
9/15/21	Note 1 Interest earned	$20,833.33		$291,666.67
10/15/21	Note 1 Interest earned	$20,833.33		$312,500.00
11/15/21	Note 1 Interest earned	$20,833.33		$333,333.33
12/15/21	Note 1 Interest earned	$20,833.33		$354,166.67
1/15/22	Note 1 Interest earned	$20,833.33		$375,000.00
2/15/22	Note 1 Interest earned	$20,833.33		$395,833.33
3/15/22	Note 1 Interest earned	$20,833.33		$416,666.67
4/15/22	Note 1 Interest earned	$20,833.33		$437,500.00
5/15/22	Note 1 Interest earned	$20,833.33		$458,333.33
6/15/22	Note 1 Interest earned	$20,833.33		$479,166.67
7/15/22	Note 1 Interest earned	$20,833.33		$500,000.00
8/15/22	Note 1 Interest earned	$5,066.67		$505,066.67
8/15/22	Note 1 Interest Paid		$3,400.00	$501,666.67
9/8/22	Promissory Note 2 (Note 2) W/ ($42,000) paid on 12/15/22	$35,000.00		$536,666.67
9/20/22	Note 1 Interest earned	$5,066.67		$541,733.33
9/20/22	Note 1 Interest Paid		$3,400.00	$538,333.33
1020/22	Note 1 Interest earned	$5,066.67		$543,400.00
10/20/22	Note 1 Interest Paid		$3,400.00	$540,000.00
10/20/22	Note 2 Interest Earned	$2,333.33		$542,333.33
11/20/22	Note 1 Interest earned	$5,066.67		$547,400.00
11/20/22	Note 2 Interest Earned	$2,333.33		$549,733.33
11/29/22	Note 1 Interest Paid		$3,400.00	$546,333.33

DATE	DESCRIPTION	CREDIT	DEBIT	ACCOUNT BALANCE
12/15/22	Note 2 Closed		$42,000.00	$504,333.33
12/15/22	Promissory Note 3 (Note 3) W/ ($50,500) paid on 6/15/23	$42,000.00		$546,333.33
12/20/22	Note 1 Interest Earned	$5,066.67		$551,400.00
1/20/23	Note 1 Interest Paid		$3,400.00	$548,000.00
1/20/23	Note 1 Interest Earned	$5,066.67		$553,066.67
1/20/23	Note 1 Interest Paid		$3,400.00	$549,666.67
1/20/23	Note 3 Interest Earned	$1,400.00		$551,066.67
2/20/23	Note 1 Interest Earned	$5,066.67		$556,133.33
2/21/23	Note 1 Interest Paid		$3,400.00	$552,733.33
2/20/23	Note 3 Interest Earned	$1,400.00		$554,133.33
3/20/03	Note 1 Interest Earned	$5,066.67		$559,200.00
3/21/23	Note 1 Interest Paid		$3,400.00	$555,800.00
3/20/23	Note 3 Interest Earned	$1,400.00		$557,200.00
4/20/23	Note 1 Interest Earned	$5,066.67		$562,266.67
5/15/23	Note 1 Interest Paid		$3,400.00	$558,866.67
4/20/23	Note 3 Interest Earned	$1,400.00		$560,266.67
5/20/23	Note 1 Interest Earned	$5,066.67		$565,333.33
5/30/23	Note 1 Interest Paid		$3,400.00	$561,933.33
5/20/23	Note 3 Interest Earned	$1,400.00		$563,333.33
6/20/23	Note 1 Interest Earned	$5,066.67		$568,400.00
6/20/23	Note 1 Interest Paid		$3,400.00	$565,000.00
6/20/23	Note 3 Interest Earned	$1,400.00		$566,400.00

Paul Thomas Croft <paul@croftenterprisesllc.com>   Fri, Sep 15, 2023 at 4:52 PM
To: Paul Thomas Croft <paul@rhinoonward.com>
Bcc: pmdougherty1@gmail.com

I'm Paul Croft, majority shareholding of ROI.

There have been a lot of conversations surrounding the closing of our accounting firm, Croft & Frost. I want to be the first to tell you that ROI and the investment subsidiaries are separate entities from Croft & Frost.

We continue our diligent work to get this deal closed for all our investors. We have also enlisted the help of a few of the major investors, to help get this deal across the finish line.

We are meeting as a group this weekend and will set up calls next week to inform our investors on status.

My apologies for any concerns the closing of Croft & Frost has caused.

We have reason to be confident that the deal will get done.

ONWARD,

-Paul T. Croft
Founder, Executive Chairman & Majority Shareholder

To: Investors of ROI

From: Paul Croft (majority equity owner of ROI)

Date: October 13th, 2023

RE: Update: 10.13.23

Dear Investors of ROI:

Please accept this letter as my continued effort to be transparent with you regarding the latest with ROI.

One, I do not have the financials for ROI yet. I continue to seek these so we can all understand the current state of the investments.

Two, as some of you already know and with no intent to be braggadocious, my skill set is best utilized in forging connections amongst people, sharing a vision that is mutually beneficial, inspiring others to believe in that vision and working tenaciously to achieve that vision by placing people in the right position. To that end, I am the first to say I am not qualified to manage the production of a hydrogen facility plan. The breadth and scope of the technology involved is beyond my education. This is why ROI had a management team in place and needs new day in, day out operators to carry this company forward. In addition, I am the first to say I am not qualified to handle the bookkeeping and accounting for a company such as ROI. Its why ROI had that those services in place.

I have been back with the Company for 30 days now. Over the last weeks, I have stepped into what I do best by attempting to secure investments and/or financing to help ROI secure new, more competent management to get the aforementioned fully executed funding contracts to fruition. There are some interested investors but until I have a legal agreement fully executed, I cannot claim it's been achieved. In football terms, I believe we're approaching the red zone. What I do best will certainly be a key component for ROI to keep moving forward. I hope to deliver some good news on this front in the upcoming weeks.

Pat Dougherty

RE: Update: 10.20.23

Dear Investors of ROI:

Please accept this letter as my continued effort to be transparent with you regarding the latest with ROI.

I understand that the former CEO of ROI, ████████████ has stated that ROI spent $1.8 million on the Company. I have been away from the company for the last year but I do want all of you to know that JD Frost and his accounting team drafted a 2022 tax return that shows nearly 8x times that was spent on ROI.

In terms of ROI moving forward, I continue to be in discussion with potential investors to help ROI secure funding for new management. I am consumed with ROI and doing everything I can to keep this company moving forward.

Sincerely,

Paul Croft

126

RE: Update: 10.27.23

Dear Investors of ROI:

Please accept this letter as my continued effort to be transparent with you regarding the latest with ROI.

I am pleased to report that I had a positive meeting with potential investors in ROI over the last week. I am reluctant to share more until the terms become memorialized. However, I will share that these potential investors see the vision, financial upside and disruptive market force behind a hydrogen facility.

I know a lot of you are concerned about ROI based largely on what happened at the accounting firm of Croft & Frost. Please understand that ROI is distinct from Croft & Frost. I continue to maintain a steadfast belief that ROI will flourish. The mission, technology and strategy involved is at the forefront of a new chapter for our country and world.

Sincerely,

Paul Croft

Dear Investors of ROI:

Please accept this letter as my continued effort to be transparent with you regarding the latest with ROI.

I continue to work hard on keeping this Company afloat and moving forward. Certain articles by the press lumping ROI with the issues that plagued the accounting company of Croft & Frost have slowed down the funding process. As I've explained to all of you, ROI is a separate entity from Croft & Frost. Two separate entities with two separate missions. I've explained this to potential investors to alleviate their concerns. In addition, to help address the concern that these funds will be used to bankroll anything other than ROI, I am more than open to placing the funds in a trust requiring oversight and approval before being released for legitimate ROI expenses. I am putting a lot of effort into ROI for all of us. I do feel bad that the company hit a rocky road while I was away on leave and desperately want to make the company thrive to benefit us as a whole.

I will not have an update next Friday due to the Thanksgiving holiday. My next update will be on 12.1.23.

Sincerely,

Paul Croft

To: Investors of ROI

From: Paul Croft (majority equity owner of ROI)

Date: December 1st, 2023

RE: Update: 12.1.23

Dear Investors of ROI:

Please accept this letter as my continued effort to be transparent with you regarding the latest with ROI.

Unfortunately, I do not have the news I wanted to share in this letter post-Thanksgiving. I remain in active discussions with potential investors. In fact, I am currently in the northeast engaging in these discussions in person, day and night. I am working hard on securing additional investment funds in ROI to keep the company moving forward. I hope to have some good news on this front shortly.

Sincerely,

Paul Croft

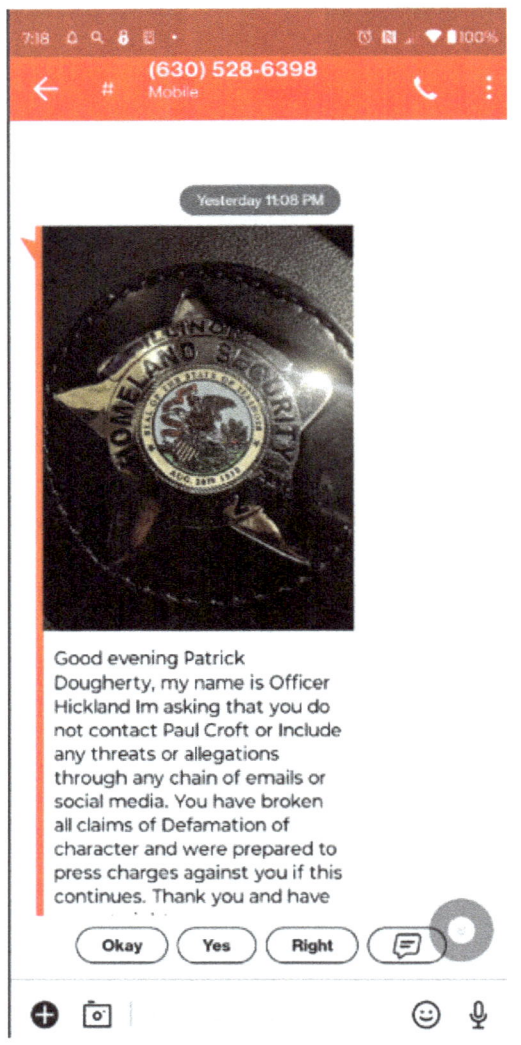

7:18

(630) 528-6398
Mobile

Yesterday 11:08 PM

Good evening Patrick Dougherty, my name is Officer Hickland Im asking that you do not contact Paul Croft or Include any threats or allegations through any chain of emails or social media. You have broken all claims of Defamation of character and were prepared to press charges against you if this continues. Thank you and have

Okay   Yes   Right

a great night.

Elements of "Defamation of Character"
To prevail on a claim for defamation of character, a plaintiff must prove(we have proof) four specific elements:
1 You made a false statement about the plaintiff. The plaintiff has the burden of proving that the statement was false.
2 The statement was made publicly, meaning it could not be in a private conversation between you and the plaintiff. In addition to establishing that others heard or read the statement, the plaintiff must prove that it could be reasonably interpreted as disparaging.
3 You acted with malice, or with negligence as to the falsity of the statement. The plaintiff must prove that you knew, or should have known, that the statement was false and was likely to cause harm to the plaintiff.

4 The plaintiff suffered actual damages as a result of the statement. This means damages that can be expressed in monetary terms and are directly attributable to the statement.

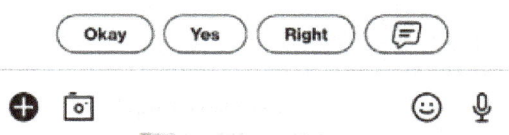

References

www.DuluthMonitor.com

https://www.rhinoonward.com/

www.TruthFinder.com

Chattanooga Times Free Press

https://www.pressreader.com/usa/chattanooga-times-free-press/20240227/281513641095042

https://www.tuftco.com/

Cornell University Legal Information Institute

https://www.law.cornell.edu/wex/ponzi_scheme#:~:text=Ponzi%20schemes%20are%20a%20type,business%20activity%20that%20produces%20revenue.

www.Forbes.com

https://www.youtube.com/watch?v=ej1k4GZLiWU

www.cbsnews/chicago

https://www.cbsnews.com/chicago/news/croft-frost-chicago-businessmen-fraud-claim/?intcid=CNM-00-10abd1h

https://en.wikipedia.org/wiki/Bernie_Madoff

www.ingramcontent.com/pod-product-compliance
Lightning Source LLC
LaVergne TN
LVHW022206010825
817715LV00032B/489